Voices Against Domestic Violence

Voices Against Domestic Violence

Biblical, Theological & Sociocultural
Appraisal of the Experiences of the Oppressed
Tribal, Children, Men & Women

Edited by
A. Tali Ao

Foreword by
Takatemjen

Clark Centre for Peace Research and Action (CCPRA)
Clark Theological College

&

Christian World Imprints®

CCPRA Publication Series No. 8

First Published in 2016 by

Clark Centre for Peace Research and Action (CCPRA)
Clark Theological College
Aolijen, Mokokchung 798601 / Nagaland
ctcprin@gmail.com
www.ctcnagaland.com
Phone: 09436006979

&

Christian World Imprints™
Christian Publishing & Books from India
H-12 Bali Nagar, New Delhi-110015
info@christianworldimprints.com
www.ChristianWorldImprints.com
Phone: +91 11 25465925

ISBN: 978-93-5148-135-5 (HB)
ISBN: 978-93-5148-136-2 (PB)

Printed at Replika Press Pvt. Ltd.

Contents

Foreword

The Clark Centre for Peace Research and Action (CCPRA) has conducted over a dozen seminars on Conflicts and Peacebuilding during the last 6 years since its inception. Most of the seminar papers have been collected and published by the Centre. The present volume is the eight one in its Publication series. I am happy to note that we have achieved our vision and mission in several ways through these seminars and publications. One of our achievements is that we were able to involve the academia - scholars from the universities in almost all the seminars we have conducted so far. Their presence in our seminars have greatly enhanced and enriched our interaction and discussions and the quality of the final product of paper writing.

The present volume deals with the issue of Domestic Violence which has become a national as well as a worldwide problem today. Realising the problem and the issues related with Domestic Violence, the CCPRA organised a seminar in November 2014. All the papers published here were presented in that seminar. I thank Dr. Tali Ao who has edited this volume. I am also grateful to the Christian World Imprints, New Delhi, who has agreed to go into a joint venture with Clark Theological College in terms of publishing our books. I hope this partnership will go a long way and bear much fruit. I would also like to express my gratitude to the participants of the seminar and especially the paper readers. And last, but not the least, I would like to acknowledge the support and generous contribution of EMW, Germany, since 2011. Had it not been for the support and encouragement of Dr. Michael Biehl and his colleagues, the work of CCPRA would not have come this far. Thank you friends!

May the good Lord bless all of you who read this book. And may you become a channel of peace in your home and in your workplace.

Takatemjen
Principal
Clark Theological College
Aolijen
February 11, 2016

Acknowledgements

At the outset, I express my sincere gratitude to the members of the CCPRA Committee, CTC, for reposing their trust on me by giving me the honour to edit this book on behalf of the Committee. Particularly, my thanks go to Rev. Dr. Takatemjen, the Principal of the College and Advisor to the CCPRA who gave me all the encouragements and for connecting me with Christian World Imprints (CWI), Delhi to publish the book; also for making all the other necessary contacts and arrangements. I am also grateful to him for showing his kindness in writing the Foreword for the book.

Secondly, I am thankful to all the paper writers for their painstaking labour of love. All of them happily accepted our invitation to write the papers, present and revise them for publication. I cannot remember all the participants of the seminar on domestic violence, whose names are too numerous to mention here. They all deserve deep appreciation for all their comments, suggestions, inputs and the insights on the subject.

Thirdly, Mr. Zülunüngsang, the former CCPRA Co-ordinator deserves a special appreciation for all the works he did to make the seminar a great success and Ms. Pursenla, the present Co-ordinator of CCPRA, for seeing through the papers getting published.

Fourthly, the CWI and its prompt, efficient staff members and their international class publication workmanship are highly appreciated. I am sure our partnership in this venture will continue for many years to come. Also, a big thanks to the CWI staff for coming up with a fine and fitting cover design for the book.

Finally, our profound appreciation and thanks go to the EMW, Germany, for their unflinching support and sponsoring this publication and other publications and peace actions of CCPRA since its inception. The members of the EMW are truly the champions of peace initiatives not only in their land but even beyond the boundaries and barriers that may stand on the way to peace, justice and love. May God bless and increase their priceless efforts.

The Editor

Introduction

A. Tali Ao

It is said that family is a great 'shock absorber'. The irony is that many shocking things also happen in the family which are not easily absorbed; things which sadly are often literally home-grown. Christian family is designed to be the safest place on earth and nearest to heaven. It is a divinely instituted relational space in which every member of it should give and receive love, care and security otherwise not found elsewhere. It is a divinely ordained, religiously and socially sanctioned sacred space within which the most intimate human relationships are shared and fostered mutually by its members. It is the abode where love and affection is to be born, nurtured and allowed to flourish without any inhibition.

However, very often different forms of domestic violence ruin many families. Domestic violence may be a very subtle form of an unkind word or overtly abusive daunts or acts. One way or the other such forms of violence shatter the warmth and intimate family relationships. Such subtle or overt domestic violence may not at once break up the family and pull apart the intimate wife-husband, mother-father, parent-children relationships. But a seemingly little tempest in the form of hurt of sentiments may ruin the warmth relationship and rob its members of the spirit of belongingness, happiness, joy and all the ingredients that are required to make a happy Christian home and guard and sustain it through ups and downs in life.

Domestic violence in its multi layered and its complex form is a neglected subject and not often seriously discussed in academia. Thus, the essays in this volume in your hand deal with questions such as what domestic violence is, its root causes, and issues, questions and concerns. The articles also provide understanding, strategies of intervention in order to deal with, prevent and resist such violence. The essays have been first presented at the Seminar on: "One Voice Against Domestic Violence," organized by the Clark Centre for Peace Research and Action (CCPRA), CTC, Aolijen, Mokokchung held on the 11th and 12th November, 2014 and have been slightly revised for publication.

Highlights of the Chapters

Domestic violence by its very nature is complex and protracted phenomenon and touches all aspects of family life, especially the most inner life of its members. This requires a multiple and inter-disciplinary approach to really understand in all its depth and dimensions and to bring healing. Often it is difficult to get a once and for all solution to the kind of domestic violence at a certain point of time in a given socio-cultural and geographical location. The articles in this volume are not a panacea to all or even a single domestic violence. But each of them looks at the problem from different angles and throws light on the problem for the readers to give a serious thinking and to work to counter and overcome it. An advantage of a collection of articles in a single volume is that the reader is given a platform and an opportunity to look at the problem from various angles and provide insights to understand the issues and problems involved.

Thus, the first three chapters offer some biblical understandings of domestic violence. They also provide the reader with some perspectives on re-reading the Bible in relation to domestic violence. The first chapter deals with some aspects of domestic violence as reflected in the OT law codes. The writer, K. Lallawmzuala pays special attention to the OT laws that give legal protection to some of the most vulnerable sections in society; namely, domestic slaves, servants and labourers. Then the second chapter by Meyijungla deals specifically with domestic violence against girls, women and wife in the OT. She looks at the problem by exploring some select passages from a feminist reading of the Bible. Then the third chapter by A. Tali Ao deals with Jesus' teaching against domestic violence as reflected in the Gospels with special reference to the Sermon on the Mount, the Gospel of John and the first epistle of John.

The rest of chapters in the volume delve into the prevalence of domestic violence in the contemporary situations. A particular interest and focus of the writers in these sections is the role of patriarchy in general and the Naga patriarchal tribal customary laws and practices in particular which are responsible for much of the domestic violence especially against women and girls and other weaker sections. Thus, chapter four is an appraisal of domestic violence by Mhonyamo. He discusses the meaning and occurrences of domestic violence and its effects on the individual, family and society. The writer argues that legislation alone cannot help in bringing the change required. He thus calls for a strong commitment of people from social, political, and religious spheres to create a culture where acts of domestic violence become totally unacceptable.

The fifth chapter by Toshimenla, a sociologist, deals with the linkages between domestic violence and the patriarchal social system and mindset. She affirms that domestic violence is a social phenomenon that cuts across all sections of society driven by the values of patriarchy. She convincingly argues that domestic violence in a given society appears more as a result of tacit acceptance by the society of men's domination of women. Thus, the writer calls for a change of traditional attitude of male superiority and female subordination which requires a reassessment of deep seated patriarchal attitudes entrenched in various institutions and norms that allow for the perpetuation of male domination over their female counterparts.

The sixth chapter by L. Imsutoshi Jamir investigates into the domestic violence in tribal society against the backdrop of tribal customary laws and practices vis-a-vis the culture of silencing the victims of domestic violence. The writer calls for deconstruction of some of the Naga customary practices with a view to overcome violence, specifically the culture of silencing which has a particular and dramatic effect on the victim of domestic violence. In a similar line, the seventh chapter by Atungo Shitri briefly points out several lacunae in the Naga customary laws which further complicate the issues and questions related to domestic violence and that adds more fuel to the fire of violence at home. He rightly calls for an in-depth empirical research into the nexus between customary laws and domestic violence.

Chapter eight is by Elizabeth Imti who is a young promising sociology scholar. Although not a participant in the seminar, when she was asked for an article, she willing made available a fine piece of writing on the subject under consideration. In her article, she demonstrates the ill effects of domestic violence on emotional, mental, physical and social health of the victims especially the girls and women. She incisively and convincingly argues that domestic abuse is a direct offshoot of the gender imbalance in the patriarchal Indian culture. She rightly says that men have always been encouraged to keep their women folks under control. She cogently argues with relevant statistics and data that domestic violence can lead to unwanted pregnancies, pregnancy complications, miscarriages, early labour, low birth-weight babies and maternal deaths. According to her, many surveys have shown that assaults against women actually escalate during and after pregnancy, or during arguments over family planning. Mental and physical abuse can also affect pregnancy outcomes. Stress and trauma can induce pregnancy complications. Worse than the physical pain is the emotional anguish that a victim undergoes. This scars her for life. Emotional abuse is sometimes used as a first step in objectifying and justifying violence against another person.

The ninth chapter by Razouselie Lasetso is on the impact of domestic violence on children which is a very crucial aspect within the whole range of the subject under discussion. He deals with behavioural, social, emotional, cognitive, attitudinal, physical, spiritual and other long term affects of domestic violence and suggests several intervention strategies as well.

The next article by Eyingbeni Hümtsoe-Nienu is on theological response to domestic violence. She offers a faith-based approach that will bring change, healing and peace to both the victims and the perpetrators of domestic violence. Primarily she scrutinizes the power imbalance that leads to violations of human relationships. She then points to the faith resources particularly from the framework of God's reconciling love in Jesus Christ. The final chapter by Kaholi Zhimomi is on an integrated strategies and interventions to resist domestic violence. She categorizes the strategies into those that seek to prevent/eradicate and those that react/respond which are to be guided by the principles of prevention, protection, early intervention, rebuilding the lives of victims/survivors and accountability.

All these chapters are preceded and augmented by the Keynote Address by Rev. Dr. Takatemjen. In the address he touches on some pertinent aspects of domestic violence which he elaborates briefly and some aspects are further explored in the following chapters.

Some Observations and Further Enquiry

As it often happens, it is obvious that in such collection of seminar papers over a burning topic/issue by different writers, there will be some repetitions and overlapping which are unavoidable. For example several presenters have given similar and diverse definitions of 'domestic violence' from different angles. It is also quite normal to encounter certain controversial and debatable points which may require further research and discussion. For instance, some presenters have affirmed quite firmly that domestic violence is *not caused* by frustration, stress, poverty, alcohol or drug abuse (Razosouselie Lasetso and Mhonyamo who also excludes alcohol as a cause of domestic violence). But on the other hand, Mhonyamo himself also argues that poverty can be one of the dominant factors contributing to domestic violence. This point is further endorsed by Toshimenla in her article by citing some important research and relevant data. Now with regard to abuse/misuse of alcohol as a key cause of domestic violence, I would like to draw your attention to a recent 'Public Discourse' column in *The Morung Express* (20 November 2014, p. 4). In this column, Dr. Vetso Koza, who also has done an in-depth empirical study of abusive husbands in the Naga context of Kohima writes, "The result is, contrary to the common myths, alcohol does not seem to trigger more serious incidents. Alcohol in most cases is used as an agent for abuse excuse."

The current editor felt that such differences of opinions, views, stances, nuances and research results/reports be left to the discretion of the readers' judicious judgement and further research and inquiry. However, as readers of the articles presented here will see for themselves that one point on which almost all resource persons and participants unequivocally came heavily is the patriarchal system, culture and mindset as one of the most crucial key sources of domestic violence. If further discussion and action be generated for or against the views and findings presented here and facilitate the increase of the awareness of domestic violence and address it to reduce, prevent and eradicate by various interventions, then the aim of the publication of this humble effort of CCPRA of CTC will be fulfilled to a great extent.

Keynote Address

Takatemjen[1]

The present volume contains papers presented in a seminar conducted by CCPRA in November, 2014; dealing with the issue of Domestic Violence which has become a national as well as worldwide problem today.

The WHO defines Domestic Violence as "The intentional use of physical force or power, threatened or actual, against oneself, another person, or against a group or community that either results in or has a high likelihood of resulting in death, psychological harm, deprivation". Physical injury is the most visible form of domestic violence and it includes slapping, pushing, kicking, biting, hitting, throwing objects, strangling, beating, threatening with any form of weapon, or using a weapon. However, domestic violence is not limited to physical injury only such as rape, sexual harassment, and battering, but also verbal, psychological and religious (spiritual) abuse.

Domestic Violence Against Women

The most common form of domestic violence is against women. One of the reasons for this is the patriarchal mindset that regards women as physically and emotionally weaker than men. According to United Nation Population Fund Report, around two-third of married Indian women are victims of domestic violence and as many as 70% of married women in India between the age of 15 and 49 are victims of beating, rape or forced sex. The most common causes for women stalking and battering include dissatisfaction with

1 Rev. Dr. Takatemjen is the Principal of the Clark Theological College, Aolijen, Mokokchung, Nagaland.

the dowry and exploiting women for more of it, arguing with the partner, refusing to have sex with him, neglecting children, going out of home without telling the partner, not cooking properly, or on time, indulging in extra marital affairs, etc.

Domestic Violence Against Men

Domestic violence should not be understood as violence against women only, but as gender based domestic violence as both men and women face abuse. Domestic violence against men can take many forms, including emotional, sexual and physical abuse and threats of abuse. It can happen in heterosexual or same-sex relationships.

One might be experiencing domestic violence if his partner:

- Calls him names, insults him or puts him down;
- Prevents him from going to work or school;
- Stops him from seeing family members or friends;
- Tries to control how he spends money, where he goes or what he wears;
- Acts jealous or possessive or constantly accuses him of being unfaithful;
- Gets angry when drinking alcohol or using drugs;
- Threatens him with violence or a weapon;
- Hits, kicks, shoves, slaps, chokes or otherwise hurts him, his children or his pets;
- Forces him to have sex or engage in sexual acts against his will;
- Blames him for his or her violent behaviour or tells him that he deserves it.

Domestic Violence Against Gay, Bisexual and Transgender

If a person is gay, bisexual or transgender, he might also be experiencing domestic violence if he is in a relationship with someone who:

- Threatens to tell friends, family, colleagues or community members his sexual orientation or gender identity;
- Tells him that authorities won't help a gay, bisexual or transgender person;

- Tells him that leaving the relationship means he is admitting that gay, bisexual or transgender relationships are deviant;
- Justifies abuse by telling him that he is not "really" gay, bisexual or transgender;
- Says that men are naturally violent.

Domestic Violence Against Children

Domestic violence against children and teens comes second after the violence against women in terms of number of reported cases. The reasons for this type of violence could be failure in examinations or not being at par with other children in the neighbourhood, disobeying parental advises and orders, not being socially intelligent or as active as the parents expect them to be, or not being obedient to parents. Exposure to domestic violence puts children at risk of developmental problems, psychiatric disorders, problems at school, aggressive behaviour and low self-esteem.

Violence Against Child Domestic Labourers

The taking-in of children from other households to perform domestic chores has longbeen seen in many societies as a form of surrogacy, adoption or assisting a child from a less fortunate family. In West Africa, there is a tradition of children migrating from rural to urban areas to work for others as part of their upbringing. In most of sub-Saharan Africa, exchanges of children between couples within the extended family used to be standard forms of mutual support.

In some parts of Northeast India also, there is a similar practice of bringing-in of children from other households to perform domestic chores. Many of such child domestics go to school and work for the family during free hours. The situation of child domestic labourers is usually considered by their parents to be safe since the child may live in better accommodation than at home, may eat better, and is under the care of the employers and family members. However, children in domestic labour are at the mercy of the employer and other household members. Child domestics describe the relationship as often starting well, but later on, becoming intolerant and abusive.

Under the International Labour Organisation (ILO) Convention No. 180, violent and abusive behaviour towards child domestics is designated 'worst form' of child labour. It includes extreme overwork (16-hour days are not uncommon); beating, whipping, pulling hair, scalding with water or an iron, and denial of food. The psychological violence includes shouting, name calling, insults, threats, and obscene language.The girls are often subjected to sexual harassment, and sometimes rape leading to pregnancy. Physical health consequences can also arise from lack of food, and failure to look after injuries or treat sickness.

In the Philippines and Peru, almost all child domestic workers reported that they had suffered maltreatment consisting of physical punishment, discrimination, humiliation and sexual harassment. In Fiji, eight out of ten domestic workers reported that their employers had sexually abused them. Research in ElSalvador found that 66% of girls in domestic service reported having been abused, and that the threat of sexual advances from employers or visitors was always present. In a local study in the United Republic of Tanzania, 43% of child domestic labourers reported being beaten, insulted, denied food, fined for damages, or forced to remain out of doors. In Nepal, children frequently start work at the age of 8 or 10, and if the employer becomes annoyed with the girl and abusive towards her, she may arbitrarily transfer the girl to another household. Such children lose touch with their families entirely.

One of the most painful experiences for child domestic labourers is that of being consistently treated as an inferior being; of having no friends or social peers, not being able to play even with the employer's children. These experiences leave children with deep feelings of inferiority and chronically low self-esteem.

Violence Against Domestic Workers

> *I would wake up to start cooking, then cleaning, washing clothes, and then cooking again. No rest, there was just no rest... Because she kept yelling, I cried and asked to go back to [the recruitment] agency, but madam said 'I already bought you.'*

This is how Farah S., a 23-year-old Indonesian domestic worker in Dubai (the name is changed for her security) described her typical working day. Before she fled her employer, she said, she had to work for a household of 20 people for 21 hours a day, with no rest or day off. Her employer never paid her for the three months that she worked before she left her job.

As many as 100 million people around the world work in someone else's home.The vast majority – 83 per cent according to ILO figures – are women, many of whom are unprotected by labour laws or any form of social security. Unable to join trade unions, these women are left vulnerable to exploitation, racist and sexist abuse, beatings, food and sleep-deprivation, forced labour, trafficking, rape and even murder. Many are underpaid or unpaid in circumstances that are little more than modern-day slavery. Abuse is rarely reported and when it is, it usually goes unpunished.

Roles of the Church and Society in Curbing Domestic Violence.

Victims of domestic violence respond to their plight in different ways. Some decide to take the silent approach. Though the problem is there, they remain silent for the sake of children. Others just accept violence as part of life. They see some hope in the cycle of violence. A third group of people opt for the coercive approach, that is to say, confronting the perpetrator of violence resulting in divorce. It must be noted here that violence almost never changes without intervention. Consequently, somebody must act. Otherwise, violence will go on and the victims of violence will continue to suffer.

The church has a great role to play and a great ministry to offer to homes and families where the members suffer because of violence. The support of the church is extremely important in such situations. Professional counselling is needed for such families. Counselling centres should be established in the region aimed at helping the victims of violence and also the abuser. And in this ministry of transforming the victims and the abused, the church can take a lead.

Apart from the church, the NGO's and the government have a great role to play. The govt has the power to pass legislation for the protection of domestic workers against domestic violence and exploitation. They can develop laws and policies that would protect women against physical and sexual violence. This is already happening in some parts of the world. And this would appear to be an important solution to the problem.

Laws may come and laws may go, but if the minds of the people are not changed, nothing will change at the end of the day. And therefore, seminars like the one mentioned, should be able to study and recommend as to what really causes violence in our society today. What are the dynamics at work and tensions in our society that are causing the problem of domestic violence? Are there social inequalities of power and rights between individuals in a society that is causing the problem? These questions require an academic answer. Without this approach there can be no lasting solution to the problems we are addressing today.

Bibliography

Ahlawat, Neerja (2006). "Violence Against Women: Voices from the Field" in Manjit Singh, D. P. Singh (ed.) *Violence: Impact and Intervention*, New Delhi: Atlantic Publishers and Distributors (P) Ltd.

Alkhateeb, Sharifa, Ellis, Sharon and Fortune, Marie M. (2003). "Domestic Violence: The Responses of Christian and Muslim Communities"*Journal of Religion and Abuse*, pp. 2, 3-24.

Kalindi, Muzumdar, "Dowry related violence: An overview?"*The Indian Journal of Social Work* , Vol. 62, Issue-3, pp. 397-414, 2001.

Manju, Pawar, "Violence against women: Reasons Role and Recommendation" in D. P. Singh, Manjit Singh, (ed.), *Violence : A Concern For Peaceful Co-Existence, Bureau Publication*, Punjabi University, Patiyala, 2008.

Venning, Philippa (2010). "Marrying Contested Approaches: Empowerment and the imposition of International Principles: Domestic violence case resolution in Indonesia", *Journal of Development Studies*, Vol. 46, No. 3, pp. 397-416, March, 2010.

Visarea, Leela; Nishi Mitra; V. Poonacha and Divya Pandey, *Domestic Violence in India: A Summary Report of Three Studies,* Washington, DC, International Centre for Research on Women, 1999.

Wyche, Karen. African American Muslim Women: An Invisible Group. *Sex Roles,* 51(5- 6), pp. 318-328, 2004.

Webliography

https://en.m.wikipedia.org/.../domestic_...

www.youthkiawaaz.com/.../domestic_...

https://en.m.wikipedia.org/.../domestic_...

www.youthkiawaaz.com/.../domestic_...

www.mayoclinic.org/healthy-lifestyle/adult-health/in-depth/domestic violence-against-men/art 20045149

www.hrw.org/report/2003/02/20/violence against...

https://www.admiralty/lawguide.com/conven/seafarershours1996.html

https://www.hrw.org/news/2014/12/18/end-exploitation-domesticworkers-gulf

www.thehindu.com/news/national/karnataka/violence-against-domestic-workers-brushed-under-the-carpet/article4485465/

www.csvr.org.2a/index.phb/publications/1589-the-best-kept-secret-violence–against-domestic-workers

www.unicef.org/sowco7/docs/sowco7_panel-2_1.pdf

www.hrw.org/legacy/english/docs/2007/02/20/global15343.txt.htm

www.antislavery.org/includes/documents/cm_docs/2009c/...

1

Domestic Violence and the Old Testament

K. Lallawmzuala[1]

Introduction

This paper represents an attempt to bring out certain issues relating to domestic violence and to indicate the Old Testament concerns for domestic violence as reflected in the Old Testament law codes. An attention will be given to the Old Testament laws that deal with legal protection for one of the most vulnerable sections in society in the domestic context, namely domestic servants. We will first look at the definitions and forms of domestic violence in the present global context, and then move on to see the Old Testament perspective on this issue.

1. What is Domestic Violence?

Traditionally, domestic violence was narrowly defined and mostly associated with physical assault and bodily injury. According to the Merriam-Webster dictionary definition, for instance, domestic violence is: "the inflicting of physical injury by one family or household member on another; also: a repeated/habitual pattern of such behaviour."[2] Domestic violence is now more broadly defined, often but not always including "all acts of physical, sexual,

---

1 Dr. K. Lallawmzuala is Associate Professor, Department of the Old Testament, Aizawl Theological College, Aizawl.

2 "Domestic Violence" in *Merriam-Webster Dictionary* (Electronic version).

psychological or economic violence" that may be committed by a person who is a family member or a person that has been an intimate partner or spouse, irrespective of whether they lived together.[3]

Domestic violence is a pattern of behaviour which involves violence or other abuse by one person against another in a domestic context. It is used to establish power and control over another person(s) through fear and intimidation, often including the threat or use of violence. Domestic violence can take a number of forms including physical, emotional, verbal, economic and sexual abuse, which can range from subtle, coercive forms to marital rape and to violent physical abuse that results in disfigurement or death. Anyone can be a victim of domestic violence. Victims can be of any age, sex, race, culture, religion, education, employment or marital status. Although both men and women can be abused, most victims are women.

1.1. *Domestic Violence Against Woman*

Violence against women means any act of gender based violence that results in, or is likely to result in, physical, sexual or psychological harm or suffering to women, including threats of such acts, coercion or arbitrary deprivation of liberty, whether occurring in public or in private life.[4] Domestic violence is normally equated with violence against woman in the domestic context. It is also known as spousal abuse, intimate partner violence, family violence, battering or domestic abuse. Violence against woman is the most common of all domestic violence. One of the reasons for it being so prevalent may be the patriarchal mind set of the society that women are physically and emotionally weaker than men. It is stated that worldwide an estimated one out of three women was beaten, coerced into sex, or otherwise abused in their lifetime, usually by a member of their own

3 "Domestic Violence" http://en.wikipedia.org/wiki/ (accesed on 4/11/2014).

4 UN Declaration on the Elimination of Violence Against Women (December 1993, http://www.unhchr.ch/huridocda/huridoca.nsf/(Symbol)/A.RES.48.104.En?Opendocument).

family or an acquaintance.[5] Clearly, many women suffer as a result of ongoing domestic violence.

According to United Nation Population Fund Report, around two-third of married Indian women are victims of domestic violence and as many as 70 per cent of married women in India between the age of 15 and 49 are victims of beating, rape or forced sex.[6] National Crime Records Bureau reveals that a crime against a woman is committed every three minutes, a woman is raped every 29 minutes, a dowry death occurs every 77 minutes, and one case of cruelty committed by either the husband or relative of the husband occurs every nine minutes.[7] In India, bride burning or dowry killing is common and it is a form of domestic violence in which a married woman is killed at home by her husband or husband's family due to their dissatisfaction over the dowry provided by her family.

1.2. *Domestic Violence Against Children*

Other vulnerable victims of domestic violence are children. Violence against children or child abuse is defined by the WHO as: "Child maltreatment, sometimes referred to as child abuse and neglect, includes all forms of physical and emotional ill-treatment, sexual abuse, neglect, and exploitation that results in actual or potential harm to the child's health, development or dignity. Within this broad definition, five subtypes can be distinguished – physical abuse; sexual abuse; neglect and negligent treatment; emotional abuse; and exploitation."[8] Physical abuse is the infliction of physical injury through punching, beating, kicking, biting, burning, shaking, or otherwise harming a child. Physical abuse is generally a wilful act. Sexual abuse includes fondling a child's genitals, intercourse, incest, rape, sodomy, exhibitionism, and commercial exploitation

5 Melissa J. Doak, *Child Abuse and Domestic Violence* (Detroit, New York etc: Thomson Gale, 2007), 1.

6 Ankur Kumar, "Domestic Violence in India: Causes, Consequences, and Remedies" http://www.youthkiawaaz.com (accessed on 1/11/2014).

7 "India tackles Domestic Violence," BBC News. 27/10/206. Retrieved 25 April 2012.

8 "Child Maltreatment" http://www.who.int/topics/child_abuse/en/ (accessed on 4/11/2014).

through prostitution or the production of pornographic materials. Child neglect is an act of omission characterized by failure to provide for the child's basic needs. Neglect can be physical, educational, or emotional. Physical neglect includes failure to provide food, clothing, and shelter; refusal of or delay in seeking health care (medical neglect); abandonment; inadequate supervision; and expulsion from the home or refusal to allow a runaway to return home.

In India, this form of violence is second in terms of number of reported cases after the 'violence against women'.[9] In rural and urban India, child abuse could be widely seen in the form of child labour. Domestic violence against girls is in fact more severe at homes than boys. As the common mentality Indians prefer to have at least one male child after marriage, the girls in most of the occasions are cursed and assaulted. This kind abuse is prevalent both in cities and villages but is more common in latter case. Then there are cases of paedophilia causing sexual harassment of children in homes by family member themselves. In fact, the number of rape cases of prematured girls has been rising since last few years.[10]

1.3. *Domestic Violence Against Maids/Servants*

One of the other forms of domestic violence is ill-treatment of servants and maids in households. Tens of millions of women, boys and girls around the world are employed as domestic workers in private households. They clean, cook, care for children, look after elderly family members, and perform other essential tasks for their employers. Despite their important role, they are among the most exploited and abused workers in the world. They may be locked within their workplace and subject to physical and sexual violence. Children and migrant domestic workers are often the most vulnerable. In many homes, domestic servants are deprived of their salary and basic necessities. They are harassed and beaten and to work without even taking adequate rest. Similarly maids are often molested and raped by males in the family. Atrocities against small children working as servants are common and increasing.

---

9 Ankur Kumar, "Domestic Violence in India."

10 Ibid.

Domestic violence against maids/servants is on the increase in various countries. According to Human Right Watch, many migrant and domestic workers still face abuse and exploitation in Middle Eastern and Asian countries because governments have failed to adopt measures needed to protect them.[11] Physical violence continues to be one of the methods that is still employed against domestic workers in various homes. "There are countless cases of employers threatening, humiliating, beating, raping, and sometimes killing domestic workers," said Nisha Varia, Deputy Director of the women's rights division of Human Rights Watch.[12]

Criminal justice systems in many countries deny the human rights of domestic workers and often continue to expose abused workers to further victimization and give them no - or only severely delayed – redress. For example, in May 2008, a Riyadh court dropped charges against a Saudi employer who abused Nour Miyati, an Indonesian domestic worker, ignoring both the employer's confession and compelling physical evidence. Nour Miyati suffered daily beatings and was abused so badly that her toes and fingers were amputated after developing gangrene. During the three years of legal proceedings, she remained stuck in an overcrowded embassy shelter unable to work or return to her family in Indonesia. At one point, she also was sentenced 79 lashes for changing her testimony, though the sentence was later reversed.[13] Thousands of complaints of labour exploitation or abuse each year are received. While most involve unpaid wages, food deprivation, and long working hours with no holiday, a significant number allege verbal, physical, and sexual abuse. But many cases are never officially reported, due to domestic workers' confinement in private homes, lack of information about their rights, and employers' ability to deport them before they can seek help. Few domestic workers have access to the justice system in the countries where they work, and even those who are able to

11 "Protect Domestic Workers from Violence," http://www.hrw.org/news/2008/11/24/ (accessed on 31/10/2014).

12 Ibid.

13 Ibid.

make complaints of physical or sexual violence rarely receive redress, Human Rights Watch said.[14]

2. Old Testament Perspective on Domestic Violence

Some people have a tendency to consider the Old Testament at face value as one of the roots of domestic violence among the Christian and Jewish communities. It is believed that the way of life, based on a typical patriarchal system, promotes man as being the head of the household in the Old Testament. Man being the head of his household, who has the authority to regulate rules and values, has been exercising power over the other members of his family. Some people have a view that the ideology of the Old Testament emanated from patriarchal society, several thousand years ago and has proven it is just as powerful now as it was then. Moreover, it is also often pointed out that there are certain biblical narratives and laws that seem to endorse violence and abuse. However, it is important to remember that the OT should not be taken out of its context and interpreted without connecting to its original historical context. The OT texts were written in the contexts where there was no awareness of the modern concept of domestic violence, and were originally written to address different issues other than the modern enlightened people's concerns. It is important to see and put in place the Old Testament first in its original setting and view incidents, ideas, world views and concerns described in it from that perspective.

In fact, there are no ready-made answers from the Old Testament for many specific questions that may arise from domestic violence problems. However, from the first chapter of Genesis, we are told that man and woman are created in the image of God, which implies that there is no room for any kind of oppression and abuse as all human beings are of equal value in the eyes of God and they are given equal responsibilities in God's creation. In fact, domestic violence is in stark opposition to God's plan for families. Genesis 1 and 2 depict marriage as a one-flesh, helping relationship. There is no space for violence in family relationship as was originally designed by God. Every member of a family is valued. While children are commanded

14 "Protect Domestic Workers from Violence," http://www.hrw.org/news/2008/11/24/ (accessed on 31/10/2014).

to honour their parents (Exod. 20:12), children themselves are also regarded as a heritage from the Lord, offspring a reward from Him (Ps. 127:3). A home should be a place where all the members become a blessing for one another rather than a place of violence and abuse (Ps. 128).

There are many instances where we get the viewpoints of the victims of domestic violence and how to handle the miserable situation of the victims. For example, when David became a part of King Saul's household, he became a victim of domestic violence. The account of David and King Saul in 1 Samuel 18-26 is a textbook on the classic dynamics of domestic violence relationships. It also discusses safety planning, and leaving an abusive relationship. Psalm 55 also seems to have been written by a victim of domestic violence who provides a clear expression of the emotions felt by victims. The account of Abigail in 1 Samuel 25, praises the actions taken by a victim of domestic violence to protect her family from their abuser. If we read the Old Testament in the light of domestic violence issues, there can be wealth of resources to give us right direction and perspective in tackling the issue.

3. Legal Protection for Slave/Domestic Workers in the Old Testament

As elsewhere in the ancient West Asia, the existence of slavery seems to be taken for granted in Israel and it is never condemned categorically as an institution. However, the Hebrew term *ebed* often translated 'slave' means literally a 'servant' or 'worker', whereas the Akkadian equivalent means 'one who has come down' in social position.[15] Slavery did not fit well with the ideals of Israelite society, and laws were designed to reduce the number of people in slavery and protect slaves who were not actually freed. Another Hebrew term for slave *sakir* may be translated as 'hired servant' as he is a free person who hired himself out for wages. This person lacks economic resources and depends on daily work for these resources.[16] The hired servant

15 David L. Baker, "The Humanisation of Slavery in Old Testament Law," in *Ethics in Brief*, 12/4 (2007).

16 Mignon R. Jacobs, "Toward an Old Testament Theology of Concern for the Underprivileged," in *Reading the Hebrew Bible for a New Millennium: Form,*

is vulnerable to those who may attempt to withhold daily wages (Lev. 19:13; Deut. 24:15). He is also vulnerable to enslavement as a means of survival. The domestic servants were the most vulnerable section of people in the ancient Israelite society in terms of domestic violence as they had to fully depend upon the goodwill and mercy of their masters. The Old Testament laws protect these vulnerable persons from various forms of abuse and violence.

3.1. *Prohibition of Forcible Enslavement*

Forcible enslavement through kidnapping or human trafficking could be one of the main factors behind the abuse of domestic workers. No one has the right to deprive another member of the covenant community of their freedom:

> *When a person is caught kidnapping a brother, one of the people of Israel, and treats him as a slave or sells him, that kidnapper shall die, and so you will purge the evil from your midst. (Deut. 24:7; cf. Exod. 21:16)*

Old Testament law prohibits kidnapping, the main purpose of which would be to enslave free citizens or sell them as chattel slaves to others. In practice, in the tightly-knit society of Israel, a kidnapper would be unlikely to keep someone in their possession for long, or try to sell them to another Israelite. Probably they would sell them abroad as soon as possible (cf. Gen. 37:25-28), thus also depriving them of the benefits of living in the covenant community. Forcible enslaving of a free person like this is considered such a serious offence that it carries the death penalty. It is so serious because the one who has been kidnapped and sold is very vulnerable to be abused as he does not have any protection and rights. Putting the life of other in such a risky condition is one of the most serious offences which is against God as well as humanity.

3.2. *Voluntary Slavery and Bonded Labour*

The prohibition of forcible enslaving does not rule out the possibility of voluntary slavery. Occasionally serious financial difficulty could

Concept and Theological Perspective, edited by Wonil Kim et. al. (Harrisburg, PA: Trinity Press International, 2000), 214.

result in an Israelite becoming a slave, to pay a debt or provide for their family. The law insists that even voluntary slavery is only to be a limited period:

> *When your Hebrew brother or sister is sold [or 'sells himself/herself'] to you, and serves you six years, in the seventh year you shall let them go free from you. (Deut. 15:12; cf. Exod. 21:2)*

At the end of that period, they are to be provided with capital to enable a successful return to an independent life (vv. 13-15). This may be seen as an attempt to break the cycle of poverty that would otherwise quickly result in the freed person becoming a slave again. Such temporary slaves are also given the option of becoming permanent members of the household at the end of their six years' service, implying that slaves would be looked after so well that they might prefer to continue in that status rather than claim their freedom (vv. 16-17). In this kind of temporary slavery, there is no room for abuse or domestic violence against the one who is in trouble rather this is a golden opportunity for the unfortunate one to recharge and to have a fresh start in life.

Another possibility for paying off debt was bonded labour, also for a limited term. In this connection, it is emphasized that the labourer is not to be treated as a slave:

> *When your brother becomes poor beside you and 'sells' himself to you, you shall not make him serve as a slave. He shall be with you as a hired worker or temporary resident; until the year of jubilee he shall serve with you. Then he shall go from you, together with his children; and he shall return to his own clan, and go back to his ancestral property. (Lev. 25:39-41)*

The rules for bonded labour imply that they were intended for a family-head who made the agreement together with his whole family, where as temporary slavery generally applied to individuals. Limited-term slavery and bonded labour was made realistic by the Old Testament policy of interest-free loans (Exod. 22:25; Lev. 25:25-38). In the context where there was no other option for the ones who underwent bankruptcy, bonded labour with a limited-term was a chance for such a helpless family to restore their socio-economic wellbeing. Such a miserable condition should not be exploited or abused by the ones who are in a position to help out.

3.3. *Protection from Domestic Abuse*

There are two laws about slave abuse. The first concerns beating, and its essence is as follows:

> *When a man beats his male or female slave with a stick, and the slave dies from the beating, he shall certainly be avenged (Exod. 21:20)*

Beating with a stick or rod was a common method of discipline, especially for children (Prov. 10:13; 13:24; 22:15; 23:13-14). This is normally taken as rod of discipline rather than rod of violence or anger. The law assumes slaves will also be disciplined in this way, while insisting that masters are sensitive to the physical condition of their slaves and administer punishment accordingly. If they misjudge the situation or excessively use violence and a slave dies, they are to be avenged. Here, the Hebrew term *naqam* which is often translated as 'punished' should rather be taken as 'avenged', which probably implies the death penalty, which means that a master who kills his slave is treated as a murderer, and receives the same punishment as for killing a free person. Thus, the law provides strong protection for domestic servants from cruel treatment by their masters, and recognizes the life of a servant to be of equal value with that of any other human being. There is no doubt that the servants are also sometimes in need of discipline, at the same time such a discipline should not be the cause of excessive domestic violence or maltreatment of the servants with cruelty.

Another law deals with the case of a slave who suffers permanent bodily injury at the hands of his or her master:

> *When a man strikes the eye of his male or female slave and destroys it, he shall let the slave go free as compensation for the eye. And if he knocks out the tooth of his male or female slave, he shall let the slave go free as compensation for the tooth. (Exod. 21:26-27)*

This ruling may be compared with the Babylonian Laws of Hammurabi, where masters are compensated for injury to their slaves by third parties but nothing is said about compensation for the slaves themselves. In Israel, the master himself is punished for abuse of his slave, by being made to forfeit a valuable worker. What is more, the slave is to be freed, even for a relatively minor injury like loss of tooth. This is a message to the masters that maintaining discipline should not turn into excessive violence or abusive cruel act.

This pair of laws is unique in the ancient West Asia because slave abuse is considered in terms of human rights rather than property rights. Elsewhere slaves were treated as chattels, and abuse laws were designed to compensate the master for loss or damage to his property. Old Testament law, however, emphasizes that slaves are to be treated as human beings and ownership of slaves does not permit a master to kill or injure them. This is an indication that domestic violence against the most vulnerable people in the society is strongly discouraged.

3.4. *Provision for Holidays*

Among all the ancient West Asian laws known to us, only those of Israel give domestic workers the right to free time for worship and recreation. For example:

> *Six days you shall labour, and do all your work. But the seventh day is a Sabbath to the LORD your God; you shall not do any work, you or your son or your daughter, or your male and female slave, or your ox or your donkey or any of your livestock, or your resident alien who is in your town, so that your male or female slave may rest as you do. Remember that you were a slave in the land of Egypt, and the Lord your God brought you out from there... (Deut. 5:13-15; cf. Exod. 20:9-11)*

It is striking that the Sabbath is to be observed by the whole community, including domestic workers. The expression 'as you do' is significant in granting equal rights to all human beings with respect to this weekly holiday. If this point had not been emphasized, it is very likely that domestic workers would have been expected to continue their work while more privileged members of society enjoyed their holidays. The same point is made clear in regulations for observing festivals (Deut. 12:12, 18; 16:11,14).

Deprivation of resting time and imposition of long time working hours with no holiday has been a common experience of many domestic workers nowadays. They often work 14 to 18 hours a day, seven days a week, for wages far below the minimum wage. If we look back the ancient Israelite context where there was no much idea about human rights and no clear concept about domestic violence, we may be able to recognize the value of the provision for holidays provided by the Old Testament law for the most vulnerable persons like domestic servants.

3.5. *Asylum for Fugitive Slaves*

A major problem faced by slave-owners in the ancient time was how to stop slaves running away. To make this as difficult as possible, slaves in the ancient West Asia were often restrained with fetters or shackles. Many were distinguished by a distinctive hairstyle, or a mark which was branded, incised, or tattooed on their flesh. Inevitably some slaves still escaped, and rewards were offered to anyone who returned a runaway slave. The Laws of Hammurabi demanded capital punishment for anyone who enabled slave to escape or harboured a fugitive. When we turn to the Old Testament we find something completely different:

> *You shall not give up a slave to his master, who comes to you for protection from his master. Let him stay with you, in your midst, in the place he chooses in one of your towns, wherever suits him best; you shall not oppress him. (Deut. 23:15-16)*

Deuteronomy provides one of the most striking contrasts between Old Testament law and other ancient West Asian laws by prohibiting what was elsewhere a fundamental obligation (v.15). Members of the covenant community are not to return fugitive slaves to their masters, but must provide them with hospitality and a safe refuge. What in Babylon is a capital offence, in Israel is to be an opportunity for kindness and generosity. Like other marginal people, fugitive slaves could very easily be oppressed, but this is forbidden to the people of God. In a situation, where the slaves are in a very risky and dangerous position to face excessive domestic violence, they are given provisions for asylum; and the Israelite people are encouraged to unreservedly open their doors and harbour such vulnerable people rather than creating problem for them. This law may not be taken as an encouragement to break the rules for the slaves, but rather be taken as a deep humanitarian concern for the most helpless people in the society.

Conclusion

The above discussion indicates that domestic violence is a serious concern for any society as it does not have any boundary. It is important to pull together all the resources in our hands to raise one voice against it. In the light of the above discussion on the legal protection for the domestic workers in the ancient Israelite society, it appears that the Old Testament may have rich resources to tackle the issue of domestic violence. However, it is also obvious that the Old Testament literatures cannot be taken as a quick fix solution for every problem of domestic violence. Perhaps we should not be too quick to criticise the Old Testament for failing to address every aspect of our concerns. It is important to remember that the Old Testament literatures were written long before the concept of domestic violence was formally developed. At the same time, the Old Testament may be able to contribute at least certain basic principles to challenge the issue.

2

Domestic Violence Against Women in the Old Testament

Meyijungla[1]

Introduction

Since time immemorial the issue of domestic violence has been prevalent around the globe and it is ubiquitous beyond geographical, traditional, cultural, regional and religious barriers. It is also a grave concern among the Christians and thus many try seeking answers to the problem and tackling the same from the Bible. In fact, the Bible has much to say about domestic violence and many relevant passages are found which portray different forms of domestic violence and also speak against them.

Domestic violence is understood as any kind of harm/abuse caused physically, emotionally, verbally, sexually and even denial of one's basic rights using physical force, brutality, and cruelty and sometimes causing bloodshed. Merriam-Webster dictionary defines domestic violence as physical injury caused by family members on another. This kind of behaviour is also repeated or sometimes it is habitual. At times, the term 'domestic violence' is also used synonymously with 'domestic abuse' - mistreatment, manipulation, exploitation, etc. Undeniably there are many victims of domestic

---

1 Meyijungla, a former faculty member of the Witter Theological College, Wokha, presently she is on the staff of Bible Society of India, Shillong.

violence where majority of the victims are women and children, statistically.

The first section of the paper is a brief overview on feminist reading of the Bible. The second section briefly discusses some passages of the Old Testament that validates domestic violence against women from the perspective of feminist hermeneutics. In the last section, some texts from the Old Testament which highlights against Domestic Violence will be discussed.

1. Feminist Reading of the Bible

Feminist hermeneutics emerged in the 1970s as a product of second-wave feminism in the 1970s, although scholars recognize their ancestor in Elizabeth Cady Stanton, whose book *The Woman's Bible* caused controversy in the 1890s.[2] This publication was made with the need to "elaborate accurately what the Bible says about the subjugation of women."[3] Since its inception it has undergone stages of change which has emancipated and empowered women in many liberating struggles. Elisabeth Schüssler Fiorenza argues that the Bible contains model of liberation which must be claimed by women in their struggle for redemption.[4] Feminists presume that the Bible and most of its interpreters have been androcentric and therefore subject to suspicion.[5] Thus, feminist critical re-reading of the Bible seeks to uncover the lost traditions.[6] Silvia Schorer states that, "a responsible treatment of biblical tradition by women cannot

2 Rebecca Styler, "A Scripture of Their Own: Nineteenth-Century Bible Biography and Feminist Bible Criticism," *Christianity and Literature,* 57/1 (Autumn 2007), 65.

3 Bridget Gilfillan Upton, "Feminist Theology as Biblical Hermeneutics," *The Cambridge Companion to Feminist Theology,* edited by Susan Frank Parsons (Cambridge: Cambridge University Press, 2002), 98.

4 Elizabeth Schüssler Fiorenza, *Bread Not Stone: The Challenge of Feminist Biblical Interpretation* (Boston: Beacon Press, 1985), 2-3.

5 Feminist Hermeneutics of suspicion examines the assertive ideology behind the text. Fiorenza explicates the term feminist hermeneutics of suspicion does not assume the feminist authority and the truth of the Bible, but suspicious of its writers and interpreters who are male and that provide patriarchal purposes. Fiorenza, *Bread Not Stone,* 15-16.

6 Fiorenza, *Bread Not Stone,* 16.

be globalized; it cannot be uniformly defined worldwide; it can, however, be discussed globally."[7] Her statement can be understood as every context involving a different history with the Bible that has influenced the context and will continue to influence the treatment of biblical texts.

A broad consensus was reached that the historical-critical approach to biblical texts by feminist theologians can be described as liberative; their interpretations bring about the inclusiveness of women out of the patriarchal perspective of the biblical texts.[8] In both the testaments it is found that there are explicit passages on marginalization and segregation of women.[9] The feminists read the Bible with women's eyes. Women as victims of sexist oppression, their experiences, their social upbringing, their sufferings and struggles give them insights from the biblical texts by reading it in Feminist perspective. Some liberation theologians have noted that feminist reading of the Bible has indeed given important contribution to exegesis, hermeneutics, and theology.[10] It also challenges the systems that have so long been oppressive to women and their well-being, without which all the questions and problems of women will remain unanswered.

Hence, in the next section a brief overview of underlining domestic violence against women during the Old Testament times is discussed with special reference to some select narratives employing feminist hermeneutics.

2. Domestic Violence Against Women in the Old Testament

From the biblical times, the societal structure has been predominantly patriarchal where women's subjugation and violence against women are evidently indicated. Especially the Old Testament

7 Silvia Schroer, "We Will Know Each Other by Our Fruits: Feminist Exegesis and the Hermeneutics of Liberation," *Feminist Interpretation of the Bible and the Hermeneutics of Liberation,* edited by Silvia Schroer & Sophia Bietenhard (London: Sheffield Academic Press, 2003), 2-3.

8 Schroer, "We Will Know Each Other by Our Fruits," 9.

9 Elsa Tamez, "Women's Rereading of the Bible," *Feminist Theology from the Third World,* edited by Ursula King (London: Orbis Book, 1994), 190.

10 Tamez, "Women's Rereading of the Bible," 199.

projects a society where men were the heads in the family, religion and social institutions. Even in marriage institution, from the time of Abraham polygamy was practiced considering women to be subjugates to men. There are even many records of rape, abuses and other violence inflicted on women which were often overlooked or neglected. Steven Tracy precisely states:

> While patriarchy may not be the overarching cause of all abuse, it is an enormously significant factor, because in traditional patriarchy males have a disproportionate share of power... So while patriarchy is not the sole explanation for violence against women, we would expect that male headship would be distorted by insecure, unhealthy men to justify their domination and abuse of women.[11]

Below we will discuss some passages pertinent to domestic violence against women in the Old Testament.

3. Sexual Violence of Women in Deuteronomy: Deuteronomy 22:25-27; 28-29

Although in Hebrew there is no clear "legal or technical term for rape" that parallels the contemporary understandings of rape, biblical writers nevertheless have interpreted the Hebrew term as "violent, non-consensual sex."[12] In the light of sexual violence against women Lyn M. Bechtel explicitly defines rape as "an exploitative act that silences the male's feeling of vulnerability, inferiority and lack of control...by creating an illusion of power, control, dominance and superiority."[13] In Deuteronomic Laws, there are two laws which

11 Steven Tracy, "Patriarchy and Domestic Violence: Challenging Common Misconceptions," in *Journal of the Evangelical Theological Society* (2007), 580-583.

12 "The piel form of the verb ענה to depict sexual violation. Traditionally rendered 'humbled', or in some newer readings 'violated' or 'forced her to sleep/lie with him', many translators now see strong evidence for the use of the word 'rape'." Sandie Gravett, "Reading 'Rape' in the Hebrew Bible: A Consideration of Language," in *JSOT* 28/3 (2004), 280.

13 Lyn M. Bechtel, "What if Dinah is not Raped? (Genesis 34)," in *JSOT* 62 (1994), 21.

are commonly described as "rape laws".[14] Deuteronomy 22:25-27 discusses the case of a violated betrothed woman; and Deuteronomy 22:28-29 presents the case of a violated un-betrothed woman. Carolyn Pressler cites Marie Fortune, where she describes that "the heart of sexual violence as negation of the violated person's power to decide, to choose, to determine, to consent or withhold consent in the most concrete bodily dimensions."[15] In the Deuteronomic laws "rape" is portrayed as an act where women's will from consideration is eliminated and women's right to sexual integrity is erased.[16]

The Deuteronomic laws regard female sexuality as the possession of the woman's father or husband. These laws regard sexual violence or rape as involuntary adultery in the case of a betrothed woman or as a "financial injury" in the case of an un-betrothed woman.[17] The case of un-betrothed woman is termed as "financial injury" because the violator must pay the young woman's father fifty shekels and that he must also marry her and never divorce her.

Carolyn Pressler assumes four points that underlie the Deuteronomic laws concerning sexual violence of women. They are:

1. Sexual violence of women is an invasion of male legal and social claims;
2. The woman's guilt or innocence is a major issue;
3. A raped woman or girl is damaged goods; and
4. Underlying all: female sexuality is male property.[18]

The issue of sexual violence of women is widespread and many claim for justice regarding the consequences that the women face because of this practice. But often or not the cries of the rape victims

14 R. Westbrook and T. Frymer Kensky, cited by Carolyn Pressler, "Sexual Violence and Deuteronomic Law," *A Feminist Companion to Exodus and Deuteronomy*, edited by Athalya Brenner (Sheffield: Sheffield Academic Press, 1994), 102.

15 Pressler, "Sexual Violence", 103.

16 Ibid.

17 Ibid., 111.

18 Pressler, "Sexual Violence and Deuteronomic Law", 112.

for justice remain unheard due to reasons such as societal structure or in some cases the victims remain hidden because of fear of social stigma and discrimination. Rape as an act violates women's dignity and also negates women's will, deny women's right to physical and sexual integrity. Furthermore, it also causes many unexpressed traumas to the victims and the aftermath of such affects also leads to suicidal attempts and death.

4. Slandering of Women: Deuteronomy 22:13-21

This passage can be divided into two sections- vv. 13-19 (section 1) and vv. 20-21 (section 2).[19] In the first section, the husband's negative assertion on his wife is expressed which implies that the woman had sexual intercourse with another man prior to the marriage. Thus, the husband is deprived of "executive right to the woman's sexual and productive services."[20] The woman's virginity is questioned by her husband and in section 1 the parents of the woman take evidence[21] to the elders to refute the accusation made by the husband. And if the husband is found to be making false accusation against his wife then a threefold penalty is to be served: disciplining,[22] a fine of one hundred shekels of silver, and a prohibition not to divorce his wife (vv.18-19). In section 2, the penalty for the woman if she is proved to

19 Anthony Phillips, *Ancient Israel's Criminal Law: A New Approach to the Decalogue* (New York: Schocken, 1970), 115-16. A. D. H. Mayes, *Deuteronomy* (Grand Rapids: Eerdmans, 1981), 309-11.

20 Bruce Wells, "Sex, Lies, and Virginal Rape: The Slandered Bride and False Accusation in Deuteronomy," in *JBL 124/1* (2005), 42.

21 Traditionally it is of the view that in order to prove the virginity of the bride the husband was expected to find "blood-stained sheets resulting from a ruptured hymen." Eugene H. Merrill, *Deuteronomy* (Nashville: Broadman & Holman, 1994), 302-3. Hence, the blood stains would be the "signs of her virginity." Samuel R. Driver, *A Critical and Exegetical Commentary: Deuteronomy,* 3rd edition (Edinburgh: T&T Clark, 1965), 255.

22 The nature of disciplining the man is debatable where some opines that stipulated discipling of the man had to be flogging in public while some are of the view that the same punishment meted out to the woman is applicable to the man as well, i.e., stoning to death. However, in other law sections suggest that "men who falsely accused women of sexual infidelity were often flogged." Anthony Phillips, "Another Look at Adultery," *SOT* 20(1981), 9; Mayes, *Deuteronomy,* 310.

be not a virgin is to face the consequence of stoning to death in front of her father's door (v. 21).The penalties imposed on the man and woman does not match. In fact, the woman's punishment is found to be more severe.

In section A the man is found to be "slandering" against his wife and therefore he is a false accuser. The law code in Deuteronomy 19:16-21 gives declaration on how false accusation should be dealt- "...life for life, eye for eye, tooth for tooth, hand for hand, foot for foot (v. 20)." The text clearly points that the punishment received by the accuser should be same as that of the punishment he/she was trying to inflict on the victim. Bruce Wells comments "The apparent discrepancy in punishments seems to indicate significant incompatibility between the passage about the slandered bride and the law of false accusation."[23] Hence, the trial is not fair in serving different punishments to the accuser and the victim.

This passage shows Domestic Violence in the form of verbal ("slandered"), which leads to emotional abuse and also physical abuse (even to the extent of stoning to death) because the man has already taken the woman as wife and laid with her. Moreover, the woman is inflicted with heavier degree of punishment than the man which indicates biased implementation in the law.

5. Inferiority of Women as a Means of Physical Violence: Judges 19:1-30; 2 Samuel 13:1-9

In Judges 19:1-30, a story of an unnamed woman from Bethlehem who was taken a concubine by a Levite[24] of Ephraim is illustrated. Though socially her status was somewhat like a wife she had fewer rights. But she was unfaithful to him and went to her father's house in Bethlehem, Judah (v. 2). After four months the Levite went to her to persuade her and they were on their way after staying at the girl's father's house for five days. They went toward Jebus and stopped at

23 Wells, "Sex, Lies, and Virginal Rape," 45.

24 "The Levitical priesthood was highly respected in this region. His marriage to a secondary wife suggests some level of wealth." Koala Jones-Warsaw, "Toward a Womanist Hermeneutic: A Reading of Judges 19-21," in *Feminist Companion to Judges,* edited by Athalya Brenner (Sheffield: Sheffield Academic Press, 1993), 20.

Gibeah in Benjamin to stay for the night where an old man offered them to stay at his home. When they were at the old man's house, a group of wicked men shouted at the old man's door to give them the Levite to have sex with him. The old man instead offered his virgin daughter and the concubine to them but the wicked men denied. Therefore, the man took his concubine and sent her outside and she was raped and abused throughout the night. The woman went back to the house where her master was staying, fell down at the door and lay there until daylight. The next day when the master stepped out of the house he said to her to get up and go. But the woman did not answer which implies that she was dead.[25] Therefore she was put on the donkey and after reaching home the man took a knife and mutilated her body into twelve pieces and sent them to all the areas of Israel.

Phyllis Trible argues that this text clearly demonstrates the use of power by men over women where the women is victimised by power abuse.[26] The old man's suggestion to give away his daughter and the concubine indicates that women were powerless to defend even if they were to face severe harm. It also implies that sexual abuse is meant for woman even if she is of her own flesh, or a concubine. Moreover, in the patriarchal Israelite society women were regarded as inferior to men, hence the woman is seen to be solemnly obeying to what she is expected to do. Also, the narrative also indicates that both the men could not save the woman in the house. Therefore, the dignity of the women was esteemed low and basic rights such as right to life and protection were denied. This kind of domination and inferiority of women in the society is in existence in many cultures today where women are facing untold violence in different forms.

2 Samuel 13:1-19

Likewise, the narration in 2 Samuel 13:1-19 further illustrates on the inferiority and powerless of women against men. This passage narrates about a young man, Ammon, who fell in love with his half-sister, Tamar and how he rapes her by faking illness and luring her

25 The Hebrew text is not very definite on whether the woman was fully dead or "near dead." Jones-Warsaw, "Toward a Womanist," 24.

26 Phyllis Trible, *Texts of Terror* (Philadelphia: Fortress Press, 1984), 13.

into his bedchamber (vv.1-11). 2 Samuel 13 clearly illustrates the event leading to the rape and how Tamar tried to reason with her brother- "do not force me.....As for me where could I carry my shame?" (vv.12-13). But verse 14 recounts that Tamar fell prey to her brother inspite of her plea because he was physically stronger than her. Eventually, Ammon hated Tamar more than he loved her and also it led to great devastation for Tamar.

Feminist scholars have often studied the character of Tamar and the experience of rape. Mary J. Evans describes Tamar as a "beautiful, good-hearted obedient, righteous daughter who is totally destroyed by her family."[27] Pamela Cooper-White identifies that Tamar has resisted as much as she could with her "power-within" whereas Ammon has used the "power-over" to commit such a crime.[28] She further argues that the narrator has focussed to emphasise the male characters- David, Ammon, and Absalom by stating that "Even the poignancy of Tamar's humiliation is drawn out for the primary purpose of justifying Absalom's later murder of Ammon, and not for its own sake."[29] Therefore, it depicts the inferiority of women even in circumstances such as physical violence where she is overpowered by the supremacy and strength of the male counterpart.

Feminist biblical scholar Phyllis Trible has captioned this episode as "The Royal Rape of Wisdom" in her book *Texts of Terror.* Trible has objected the use of third person pronoun in referring to Tamar in verse 11 saying the "narrator hints at her powerlessness by avoiding her name"[30] indicating the "plight of the female."[31] She also further indicates that Tamar was a wise women because she has requested Ammon to ask her hand for marriage to the king which Trible ascribes as "her words are honest and poignant; they

27 Mary J. Evans, "Women," in *Dictionary of the Old Testament Historical Books,* edited by Bill T. Arnold & H. G. M. Williamson (Downers Grove: IVP, 2009), 994.

28 Pamela Cooper-White, *The Cry of Tamar: Violence Against Women and the Church's Response* (Philadelphia: Fortress Press, 1995), 7.

29 Cooper-White, *The Cry of Tamar,* 5.

30 Trible, *Texts of Terror,* 46.

31 Ibid.

acknowledge female servitude."[32] After the rape Ammon despised her and ordered her to get out of his bedchamber. But she responded that it was wrong to let her go because it was unlawful to send away virgin woman after rape since it was an order that the abuser should marry her. Moreover, even after Tamar was raped she continued to plead for justice.

In this passage, Ammon is seen to be very desperate for Tamar intensely he plots for intimate contact. It gives the message that women face Domestic Violence even at home with abusive partners who plot and stalk intimate partners, like Ammon.

The Domestic Violence against women as seen in the Old Testament is faced even today by women in our society. Therefore, it is necessary that these issues must be addressed and at the same time measures should be taken on how it can be reduced. Total eradication of this violence is of course not possible. However, approaches should be laid where women gets a platform to voice out their plights as often many become silent victims thereby inflicting in them great inner turmoil.

6. What Does The Old Testament Say About Domestic Violence?

Recognition and response to women's Domestic Violence has been a far cry for the victims because of factors such as complicated culture and traditional norms of the society, which often makes the victim silent leading to acceptance as normal and unavoidable. Many passages in the Bible speak against Domestic Violence and God's attitude towards those who are violent. Bible verses are often used to justify Domestic Violence, such as those that refer to male superiority and female's submission. For instance, Eve is seen to be disobedient to God and man, and to many a generalised symbol of womanhood that must be submissive and subject to discipline, while others disagree with this interpretation.[33] Some of the passages in

32 Trible, *Texts of Terror*, 45.

33 Carol J. Adams & Mary M. Fortune, *Violence against Women and Children: A Christian Theological Sourcebook* (New York: The Continuum Publishing Company, 1998), 92-3.

the Old Testament that advocates against Domestic Violence and address the issue of Domestic Violence are:

Domestic Violence against women or to anyone is considered as sin. Any kind of violence that God detests becomes sin. Marjorie Proctor Smith states that "domestic physical, psychological or sexual violence is a sin."[34] In Leviticus 25:17, God warns against taking advantage of one another, oppression and doing wrong against any person which is a form of Domestic Violence as it violates the Jubilee Law violating person's right and dignity of life. Sins such as lie, deceit and slandering (Malachi 3:5) are also Domestic Violence in the form of verbal abuse, false and damaging statement, psychological and emotional traumas. As in the case of Domestic Violence against women, there are cases of rape, abuse, oppressions, mistreatment and slandering which are regarded as sinful. Furthermore, the annulment of marriage vows is also regarded as sin because God despises divorce (Malachi 2:16).

In early Israel, divorce was approved to men, but the Deuteronomic law made stronger amendments in which the husband was required to give his wife a certificate of divorce and neither they were allowed to remarry (Dt. 24:1-4). Luck suggests that Deuteronomy 24:1-4 "intends to protect a stigmatized woman from further abuse by her offending first husband."[35] Additionally, Deuteronomy 22:29 and 22:19 deny the right of divorce to the man; when he had seduced a unbetroth virgin (Dt. 22:29) and when he had slandered his newly married wife (22:19).[36] But soon after the return from exile the Jewish men married non-Jewish women, Ezra and Nehemiah strongly opposed the inter-marriage because it went together by a great deal of Domestic Violence in Jewish homes especially on Jewish wives. Malachi 2:13-16 recounts on the unfaithful men of Judah who were guilty of mistreating their wives by breaking the marriage covenant. God clearly says that "I

34 Adams & Fortune, *Violence Against Women and Children,* 428-9.

35 William F. Luck, *Divorce and Remarriage: Recovering the Biblical View* (San Francisco: Harper & Row, 1987), 64.

36 Hinckley G. Mitchell, John Merlin Powis Smith & Julius A. Bewer, *A Critical and Exegetical Commentary on Haggai, Zechariah, Malachi and Jonah* (Edinburgh: T&T Clark, 1912), 56.

hate divorce...and covering one's garment with violence" (v.16). The man's violence against his wife by marrying non-Jewish women has caused divorce thus breaking the marriage covenant.[37] This passage is considered as the most "strongest and most outspoken" of the evil of divorce in the Old Testament.[38] Hence, it shows that divorce was a form of Domestic Violence against women who were abused by their husbands on violating marriage vows.

In several of the passages we find condemnation of the abusers. Psalm 11:5 explicitly states that the lovers of violence are condemned by God and abusers are punished (Zephaniah 1:9). Malachi 2:13-16 also shows that the violators of marriage vows are condemned by not accepting their prayers.

Conclusion

The Old Testament often considered as a violent book by many, in fact highlights a considerable amount of Domestic Violence against women. The reading of the biblical narratives from the perspective of feminist hermeneutics shows Domestic Violence against women are executed in the form of non-consensual physical abuse, slandering and abusing of women's dignity and rights by use of power. Hence, it is very necessary to address these issues even today to liberate the women out of these social barriers and subjugations which can be effective by rising out their voices and by claiming the truths of the Biblical texts which can serve as a liberative tool.

37 Mitchell, et al., *A Critical and Exegetical Commentary on Haggai, Zechariah, Malachi and Jonah,* 47.

38 Ibid., 56.

3

Jesus' Voice as Divine Voice Against Domestic Violence

A. Tali Ao[1]

Introduction

Biblically speaking, family is a divine institution created by God. God is the author, redeemer and sustainer of all the families. In and through Jesus, God is and will be the final arbitrator of all affaires of all the families. God is the master of the family with ultimate authority over the members and affairs of the family. He/She also empowers each member to contribute and live up to the expectation for which He/She has designed each family which also includes the daily well being of the family. God has not given up the family despite its failing, falling and faltering. He/She calls members of the family to account for their omission and commission and judges as well as gives guidance for the purposes and missions for which the family is ordained and destined. Hence, when Adam and Eve disobeyed God; Cain killed Abel; Hagar suffered envy and banishment from home at the hands of Sarah and Abraham; Joseph was abused, harassed, sold, and suffered injustice at his brothers' hands and later in the hands of the wife of Potiphar within a family setting; domestic feud between Esau and Jacob estranged them for years; David committed

1 Dr. A. Tali Ao is Senior Lecturer and HoD of the Department of the New Testament, Clark Theological College, Aolijen.

adultery and murder, and the list goes on; God in Her/His own freewill intervened time and again condemned the sins, punished the evil doers but also protected the innocent, restored the justice and the repentant and promised Her/His presence and blessing for the faithful seekers of His/Her ways and will in their family life. A detail exegesis and exposition of the characters' behaviours and reactions and God's responses in these and similar stories will reveal much insight on the various dimensions of causes and diseases of domestic violence and their healing. However, our focus here is domestic violence in the NT to which we turn now.

1. Divine Voice Against Domestic Violence and its Healing in the Synoptic Gospels

God's response to the variegated forms of violence at home between spouses and amongst the siblings forms a significant aspect of the core of salvation story of the Bible. The expression, 'he will strike your head, and you will strike his heel', generally known as the proto-evangel in Gen 3:15 is God's promise to destroy Satan and to restore harmony in God's family between God-human, wife-husband-children and the whole creation. This promise to treat and heal wound inflicted by violence at home is resounded throughout the OT and finds its culmination in the coming of Jesus Christ into the world. The birth of Jesus brings the family into limelight once again in an unprecedented manner. God in His/Her own will chose to reveal Himself/Herself in and through the family of Mary and Joseph, which indicates the important roles God assigns to husband/father and wife/mother and children and the centrality of marriage and family in His/Her plan of salvation. However, the pain and suffering that accompanied Mary and Joseph could have triggered much family feuds and violence although all of their experiences may not be attributed as domestic/family violence. But had not God intervened via Joseph's dreams, and had Joseph and Mary not managed and handled their anxiety, distressed and pressures with great care and respect for one another their story could have been turned into hate, shame and violence. In an honour-shame cultural context the gravity of psychological stress the young couple underwent and Joseph's resolve to divorce his young wife when he found her pregnant before they had sexual relationship indicate the deep fear of domestic violence in terms of public disgrace hovering above their head (Mt 1:18-19).

The story of Jesus' birth projects how God protected and saved righteous man and woman and the holy family from violence and shame (Mt 1:19). But on the other, the way many other families suffered state violence and atrocity at the hand of Herod who ordered killing of all the children in and around Bethlehem who were two years old or under (2:16), shows that violence in the family is associated and connected with powers that be outside the family circle. It is worth noting that the character of Joseph as *dikaios*, 'a righteous man' (see also the discussion on the idea of *dikaios* below) and his unwillingness to expose Mary to public shame/disgrace avoided much psychological pain and public stigma for both of them (1:19). Such character and attitude also created a holy and healthy family environment and provided a model to follow for Jesus as he grew up inheriting his father's trade as a carpenter and later committed his life for God's Kingdom concerns.

2. Jesus' Call to End Domestic Violence in the Sermon on the Mount

The Sermon on the Mount encapsulates some of the most essential ethical teachings of Jesus. For instance, peacemaking, non-violence, loving the enemies, prayer for persecutors, not to use abusive words against brothers and sisters, prohibition of lust and adultery and making unreasonable and unfair Jewish law of divorce as invalid are some of the relevant ethical injunctions for our discussion (5:9, 22, 27-30, 31-32, 43-45). The bottom line is that contrary to the widespread glorification of violence in the form of personal prowess, customary laws and traditions and military conquest in human history and mythology, Jesus declared peacemakers as blessed and children of God and banned even getting angry with brothers and sisters let alone murder (5:9, 21-22). Here, Jesus obviously and unambiguously rejects religious, cultural, social, psychological, and physical violence in any form. For Jesus and his followers who may be husband, wife, parent and children, violence in any form is fundamentally abnormal and pathological.[2] It is likely that the OT's images of families as recipients and agents of God's love and blessings and the lived experiences of family violence in the strive torn socio-political and religio cultural settings of first century Palestine under the Roman colonial and the patriarchal rule of his own people impelled Jesus to envisage a renewed family of God radically changed and transformed free from all forms of violence in general and domestic violence in particular. Thus, in Jesus' eschatological vision of God's family, violence in any nature has no place. This is further elucidated when Jesus explicitly rejected divorce, 'except for sexual immorality' (19:1-9), which is our point of discussion in the next sub-section.

3. Jesus' Rejection of Mosaic Law of Divorce as Divine Rejection of Domestic Violence

The reference to 'a certificate of dismissal' in Mt 19:7 alludes to Deut. 24:1-4 that sanctioned husbands to divorce their wives at their will. A look at this Mosaic law of divorce in which a husband had right to write a certificate of dismissal/divorce on the pretext of 'something objectionable' found with his wife and could send her back to her family projects a situation in which domestic violence was made legal or sanctioned by Jewish law. Such legitimization often instil wrong notion of right and wrong and creates belief systems and societal norms which combine together produce and perpetuate an environment in which domestic violence is both created, nurtured and perpetrated.[3] In due course of time, a mind set is produced which allows the divorce and the violence it inflicted upon the victim appears rational and acceptable to the abuser and

---

2 Here I am contextualizing the views of D. W. Gill, "Violence," in D. J. Atkinson, et al., eds. *New Dictionary of Christian Ethics and Pastoral Theology* (Downers Grove, Illinois: Inter Varsity Press, 1995), 887.

3 The discussion and arguments in the following section is heavily depended on and drawn from the theoretical discussion of 'combined causation model' of domestic violence put forward by H. L. Conway, *Domestic Violence and the Church* (Secunderabad: OM Books, 2003, originally published by Authentic Lifestyle, an imprint of Authentic Media Carlist, UK in 1998), 38. She also includes some discussion on biblical views of domestic violence in Chapter Three. Our proposal here converges with hers in some points and conclusions but is different from the line of her discussion at many points.

his community. The replication of this mindset in many individuals producing similar divorce cases gradually becomes a part of what is normal in society as a whole. Once this normalization happens, it becomes difficult to challenge the occurrences of injustice and violence. Then incidents of domestic violence due to divorce and conflict in the family cease to be a wayward behaviour or violent act but are taken for granted and become a fairly typical behaviour of many members of the society. Thus, fewer and fewer people become outraged. They fail to challenge such cases when they occur. Even if people learn of an incident of domestic violence fewer people are inclined to act against domestic violence. Such society becomes apathetic and accepts and even justifies abuse of spouse, children, 'helpers', and domestic violence and divorce as normal and violence especially in subtle forms as everyday affairs of life in a family.

The Pharisees' question of divorce in Mt 19:1-9 reflects similar social reality. Therefore, what is implied by the question, "Is it lawful for a man to divorce his wife for any cause?" (v. 3) simply indicates the line of argument and an affirmative statement for divorce and all the multi layered violence it implies according to the society as nurtured by the Pharisaic philosophy of marriage and family relationship. In the sight of the Pharisees and their social value system it is lawful and normal for a husband to divorce his wife for any cause. The legalization of divorce has created a mindset of self-righteous for the abuser. Then the victims' ability to think and rethink and challenge the injustice and violence has been gradually silenced if not erased by the religious sanction and custom. The victims are made objects. The abusers have robbed the rights, dignity and identity of the victims. They are made powerless and property/objects to be exploited. Therefore, Jesus' outright rejection of the husband's right to divorce is not only a clear rejection of domestic violence perpetuated and perpetrated for generation upon vulnerable wives and her family's honour as a whole by Jewish patriarchal hegemonic rule but a challenge of the patriarchal mindset in which women in general and wives in particular have become helpless victims. He sides with the victims and reinstates the marriage and family institution to the pre-fall state of the God's original design saying 'therefore what God has joined together, let no one separate' (v. 6). For Jesus the antidote for the victims and abusers in the family violence and to restore the family to its original design is God who first created and commissioned the family for His/Her purposes and missions and to enjoy harmony and fellowship with all its benefits.

How can the family be restored to God's original design and enjoy all its benefits for all the members and overcome violence both at home and the world? The ethical values enunciated by Jesus in the Sermon on the Mount alluded briefly above is a good starting point for this question. There Jesus envisages a renewed family of God consists of children of God who are peacemakers, lovers of enemies both at home and beyond, who have renounced anger and abusive words. We can garner much insights and resources from the Synoptic Gospels as well as the rest of the NT literature for this purpose. However, for our purpose in this short paper we can turn to the fourth Gospel and 1 John to look at Jesus' vision of the family of God which should be the guiding model and principle for the earthly Christian families.

4. Jesus' Quest for the Violence Free Family of God in the Fourth Gospel and 1 John

We see two sharply contrasting families reflected in John and 1 Jn, viz., the family of God and the family of the devil. The former is brought into being by divine birth when people positively received and believed in the name of Jesus. They become children of God born not by the human 'bloods', i.e., natural procreation or out of the will of humans' societal cultural contract or the wishes and desires of the husbands but by the will of God (Jn 1:13).

By contrast, nowhere in the Bible do we find that the children of the devil are born of the devil. This is not surprising because the devils are never creative but always violent and destructive. In this regard, R. E. Brown makes an insightful observation when he says that the children of the devil in Johannine writings are nowhere said to have been born of devil. This may be a deliberate omission because the opposite of being born of God is to remain being born of human rather than born of devil.[4] The devil is in no way creative, he does

4 R. E. Brown, *The Epistles of John: Translation with Introduction, Notes and Commentary*, ABC, Vol. 30 (New York: Doubleday, 1982), 405.

not give life but takes it away (cf. Jn 10:10, 'the thief comes only to steal, kill and destroy'). People become the children of the devil not by the devil's creative act since there is no such thing of devil's nature but by their evil deeds (cf. 'everyone who commits sin is a child of the devil', in 3:8).[5] It is said that to be a child of devil is by immoral relationship while to be a child of God is more than moral behaviour because God's child is a new creation, new birth born of God's love in Jesus Christ.[6]

This leads us to explore the most essential positive aspects that contribute to the making of violent free Christian family vis-a-vis the destructive elements and works of the devil in the world. The most essential ingredients for a violent free family and the power and strength to face a society and a world torn apart with all forms of violence and war is God's love and God's will for the family as revealed in the person and work of Jesus. For the authors of the fourth Gospel and 1 John the heavenly family of God consisting Father-Son-Holy Spirit is the basis and decisive foundation for a happy family. The divine family of Father-Son-Spirit mutual relationship is the basic model for the human family relationship that aspires to live according to the leading of the Spirit. The most important aspect of this relationship is the divine love. This sharply distinguishes Christian family from devil's family if ever there is such thing as devil's family.

The life and destiny of God's children both individually and collectively rests on God's love and is constantly moulded and nurtured by His/Her grace. As such God's love and grace are the most essential ingredients of Christian family that give birth to and nurture Godly/loving wife/mother, husband/father and children. This concept of love establishes the intimate filial relationship between God and the children. This also gives birth to a loving

5 The Greek word *diabolos*, devil in Jn 6:60; 8:44; 13:2 is associated with Judas the betrayer and Jesus' arch rivals, 'the Jews'. It also occurs in Rev 2:10; 12:9, 12; 20:2, 10. The other name for devil is Satan again associated with Judas mentioned only once in Jn 13:27, but occurs 7x in Rev (2:9, 13, 24; 3:9; 12:9; 20:2, 7). We must acknowledge that violence in the family and in the society at large is linked and associated with works of Satan and sin in many ways. Cf. Stott, *The Letters of John*, 141f., for further discussion.

6 Brown, *Epistles*, 405.

relationship amongst the believers expressed by the term, 'beloved' in 1 Jn.[7] Of all the NT writings, it is the Johannine works which emphasize and give definite shape, colour and meaning to the unconditional and universal love of God.[8] Jesus' coming into the world, his death and resurrection is the revelation of God's love (Jn 3:16).[9] 1 Jn affirms this when it says, "God's love was revealed among us in this way: God sent His only Son into the world so that we might live through him" (4:9). God made Israel as His/Her child through His/Her saving acts as an expression of His/Her love. As the deliverance from Egypt and establishment of the covenant are unique salvific events (Ex 2:23-25), so also God redeems and recreates whoever put their trust in God in and through Jesus. This is a loving act which in turn demands love. Brown again succinctly summarizes the concept of love in 1 Jn saying, "*Agapē* is not a love originating in the human heart and reaching out to possess noble goods needed for perfection; it is a spontaneous, unmerited, creative love flowing from God to the Christian, and from the Christian to a fellow Christian.... Indeed, *agapē* is so totally divine in origin that twice the author claims, 'God is love' (1 Jn 4:8, 16)."[10]

The other important marks of God's children and the family of God are the demand for purity and holiness in all areas of life in view of their future hope. The theological, christological and eschatological indicatives become the basis for the Epistolary author's imperative, 'everyone who has this hope focused on him purifies himself, just as Jesus is pure" (1 Jn 3:3, NET).[11] The use of 'everyone

7 Compared to 12 Pauline uses of *agapētoi*, beloved ones in all of his 13 letters traditionally attributed to him, the six Johannine uses in 1 Jn 2:7; 3:2, 21; 4:1, 7, 11 is very high. It supports 1 Jn's link with the community of the Beloved Disciple.

8 Brown, *Epistles*, 254, says that Christians gave a new intensity and specific meaning to the idea of love.

9 E. E. Pokes rightly affirms that Jn 3:16 is the "foundational statement of the whole Gospel of John." Cited by U. Schnelle, *Theology of the New Testament*, trans. M. E. Boring (Michigan: Baker Academic, 2007), 664, n.16.

10 Brown, *Epistles*, 254f.

11 The verb, *hagnizei*, to purify is expressed in indicative, but both R. Bultmann (*The Johannine Epistles*, Trans. R. Philip O'Hara, Lane C. McGaughy and Robert W. Funk, Hermeneia [Philadelphia: Fortress, 1973, German 1967],

who has this hope' again differentiates God's children from children of devil who might not accept the hope of Christ's second coming and felt the need for purity of life as they probably thought they were sinless (1 Jn 1:8). The use of 'hope' further strengthens God's children's futuristic hope mentioned in 1 Jn 2:28. They balance, instead of contradiction, the predominant realized eschatology in Jn. This future hope is the defining factor for self-understanding and behaviour of the community members born of God's love. This links itself to the past God's revelation in Jesus, which sustains and governs the present way of life within a larger Christian community in general and Christian family in particular and enables itself to hope for greater glory at his coming again. Thus, the author is at pain to protect the integrity of the community from sin and lawlessness. He thus urges them to purify themselves after the pattern of Jesus (1 Jn 3:3, 4).

The sole use of the verb 'to purify' here may have been taken from the milieu of Jewish cultic life as its use in Jn 11:55 for purification rite suggests. However, for our author Jesus is the supreme model for the need of purification and sanctification not Jewish rites or any other religious rites which were all superseded by his life and deeds.[12] Rather the decisive norm and model for sanctification is Jesus, as the expression 'just as he is pure' attests (1 Jn 3:3; cf. 2:6). In this regard, what comes to our mind is Jesus' prayer, 'Sanctify them in the truth...And for their sakes I sanctify myself, so that they also may be sanctified in truth' (Jn 17:17, 19). Thus, right belief in Jesus, i.e., sound christology is the basis and norm for ethical life at home and in society. The attitude and lifestyle of individuals and community life, *koinōnia,* i.e., participation in all areas of life and sharing of things must correspond with, rather than contradict, the one in whom they believe as the atoning sacrifice, risen from death, the advocate with the Father and coming again to take them to be with him and the Father. This reiterates the author's frequent desire to relate indicative

---

49) and G. Strecker (*The Letters of John, A Commentary on 1, 2, and 3 John*, Trans. L. M. Maloney, ed. H. Attridge [Minneapolis: Fortress, 1996, German 1989], 91), rightly say that it has an imperative meaning.

12 R. Schnackenburg, *The Johannine Epistles: A Commentary,* Trans. T. Reginald and I. Fuller (Kent: Burns and Oates, 1992, German 1984), 161.

and imperative in actual life. Jesus is the *hagnos*, pure, i.e., he has appeared for sinners at God's command, and through his atoning death he has taken away sins (cf. 1 Jn 1:7, 9; 2:1-2; 4:10). This lays the ground for normative ethical behaviour, by which all believers, in light of the eschaton, ought to show themselves as *dikaios*, just/righteous and act justly (2:29).[13] The readers are told that being born of God and hoping to be like God/Jesus is contingent on the right belief and conduct.[14]

Conclusion

Several conclusions can be drawn from the above discussion to address issues and concerns of domestic violence and violence in general from the NT perspective:

1. The Bible has rich resources to address the growing concerns of domestic violence in our society both for believers and people who may not subscribe to Christian faith and beliefs.
2. We need to take cognizant of the use and abuse of the Bible to either endorse violence or to argue against violence as such we must take great care not to use Scriptures to validate violence of any kind.
3. The traditional ways of reading and drawing conclusion by word study is painfully limited. Along with it, an integrated and interdisciplinary way of looking at the Bible as the story of God's plan of salvation and revelation in specific sociopolitical and religiocultural contexts is important. Thus, the narrative features of the Bible and the ways human characters and manmade laws and customs project their sin and limitation and the ways God encounters them to correct or override completely and direct members of the family according to His/Her will, plan and purpose is important.

13 Strecker, *The Johannine Letters*, 92.

14 S. S. Smalley, *1, 2, 3 John*, WBC, Vol. 51 (Waco, Texas: Word Books, Publisher, 1984),148.

4. The discussion on selected passages/sections from the Synoptic and Johannine writings show that violence is sin and it is the result of sin and is associated with devil and Satan and evil works. It is identified and condemned in the Bible.
5. Glorification of violence in any form in the family and in the society cannot be justified. Any law, custom, faith and practice that endorse violence against spouses, children and 'helpers' should be challenged, condemned and be changed. Laws and customs alone cannot decide what is permissible and therefore legal rather we need to invoke the theological, christological and ethical demands as manifested in the Scriptures and laid down by the Bible.
6. The most authoritative image of God as portrayed in the NT and as revealed in and through the person and work of Jesus is a loving God who is against violence. He/She is a non-violent God. As such God's love and grace is the best antidote to violence and Jesus is the embodiment of this love. His life and teaching are the best model and guidance to address and manage violence at home and society.

4

An Appraisal of Domestic Violence

Mhonyamo Lotha[1]

Introduction

Today we live in a world where we see violence being committed everywhere. Every day we see violence take place in one form or the other. In short, one can say it has become an integral part of human race. Of the many forms, domestic violence is one such form which is a part of many families. This menace has affected the proper development of families which in the long run also affects the society. There is an urgent need to address this issue but one can see that in many cases these goes unresolved leading to a strained relation within the members of the family. Our attempt in this regard will be to look at what domestic violence is? What are the contributing factors to it and how it affects an individual and suggest some remedial measures to combat domestic violence?

1. Some Basic facts

a) The National Crime Record Bureau reveals that a crime against a woman is committed every 3 minutes, a woman is raped every 29 minutes, a dowry death occurs every 77 minutes, and cruelty committed by husband or relative every 9 minutes.

---

1 Mhonyamo Lotha, a former Lecturer at the Clark Theological College, Aolijen, in the Department of History of Christianity, presently he is pursuing his Ph.D. at the Martin Luther Christian University, Shillong.

b) The Universal Declaration of Human Rights (UDHR 10th Dec 1948) guarantees certain rights which can be related to domestic violence.
   a) Article 1 provides freedom of equality of all.
   b) Article 2 prohibits discrimination.
   c) Article 3 provides right to life and liberty.

c) The Convention on Elimination of Discrimination Against Women (CEDAW) in its general recommendation no. 19 (1989) declares that states should protect women against violence especially occurring within the family.

d) In 1983, the Indian Constitution recognized domestic violence, as a specific criminal offence under Sec 498A of the Indian Penal Code (IPC) punishable up to three years of imprisonment and a fine.

e) In 1993, the United Nations adopted Declaration on Elimination of Violence against Women.

f) In 2005, (13th Sept) Indian Constitution passed the Protection of Women from Domestic Violence Act endorsed by the four states namely Andhra Pradesh, Tamil Nadu, Uttar Pradesh and Odisha.

2. What is Domestic Violence? (Oppressor and the Oppressed)

The term domestic violence can be interpreted as violence against another in an intimate relationship such as dating and marriage. On a wider context it can be taken in the whole family unit, including violence aimed at children or the problem of 'elder abuse'. Walker Leonore defines the victim of domestic violence as a woman who is repeatedly subjected to any forceful physical or psychological behavior by a man in order to coerce her to do something he wants to do without any concern for her rights.[2]

According to Indian Child Services, domestic violence can be described as when an adult in a relationship misuses power to control another. It is the establishment of fear and control in a relationship through violence and other forms of abuse, which may include physical abuse, sexual assault and threats. Sometimes it can also take

2 Helen L. Conway, *Domestic Violence and the Church* (Secunderabad: OM Books, 2003, cited as H. L. Conway, *Domestic Violence and the Church*), 5.

the form of making someone feel worthless. The abuser tortures and controls the victim by calculated threats, intimidations and physical violence.[3]

Violence covers all kinds of physical abuse: kicks, punches, slaps, pushes, burns, use of weapons, pulling of hair, shaking, dragging, choking, biting, rape etc. It also includes verbal abuses like shouting, destruction of property, display of weapons, and actions which the victim know that it will lead to action. So a victim suffers both physical and psychological abuses. In this case, domestic violence can be closely linked to control and manipulation of the victim by the perpetrator and there are number of ways by one can accomplish this without resorting to a physical assault. One thing one to be noted in this regard is that all of these ways, however, override the rights, desires and emotions of the victim.

3. Levels of Domestic Violence

Violence is a complex phenomenon which has its roots in the interaction of many factors- biological, social, cultural, economic and political.

The first level is the biological factors that influence how an individual behaves. For example, the demographic characteristics (age, education, income), psychological or personality disorders, substance abuse, and a history of behaving aggressively or experiencing abuse.

The second level is the relationship with family, friends, intimate partners and peers, which increase the risk of being a victim or perpetrator. For example, having friends engaging in violence may increase a young person's risk of becoming a victim or perpetrator.

The third level is the community context in which social relationships occurs, such as schools, workplaces and neighbourhoods.

The fourth level is the broad societal factors like availability of weapons and social cultural norms. For example, priority of parental

3 Delores Friesen and Mary Shamshoian, "Peacemaking in the Family: A Systematic view of Domestic Violence," in *Violence and Peace*, ed. (Frampton F. Fox, cited as Friesen & Shamshoian, "Peacemaking in the Family,"), 204-205.

rights over child welfare, male dominance over women and children, etc.[4]

4. Factors that Contributes to Domestic Violence

There are many factors that contribute to domestic violence some of which are highlighted below.

a) **Economic Factors:** Poverty can be one of the dominant factors contributing towards domestic violence in the families. In a survey carried out in a locality (observatory analysis), it was found out that men who were unemployed and poor tend to lay the blame on the wives and the children. In many cases, wives were the only bread earning member in the family. The man had nothing to do than sit and talk with friends the whole day over drinks bought by friends who were a little better off. In the evening this man would go home and start abusing the wife and the children. They would often force their children to go and work as labourers and bring earnings which he would mostly spend on gambling and drinks, and if the children do not bring enough money or disagree to work, he would beat up or sometime threaten. One basic thing to be noted here is if the husband like the wife had been involved in earning bread for the family, children can have access to proper education and make them qualified persons to have a pleasant job that can support the family as a result violence at home may be reduced.[5]

b) **Alcohol and Drugs:** Alcohol and drugs are not clearly identified cause of domestic violence, though it clearly is a correlate and may be a contributing factor. Gelles and others argue that "substance abuse is not a cause of family violence-rather it is often used as an excuse for family violence." Abusive men with severe alcohol and drugs problems are just likely to abuse their families when they are sober as when they are drunk. Some

4 Uli Jager, et al., *Fostering Civic and Nonviolent Education in Jordan* (Berlin: Berghof Foundation, 2014), 70.

5 An observatory study done on a locality in Wokha, in the process of the work.

commit their worst abuse when they are sober, while others deliberately get drunk so they can justify their violence. In other words, he does not abuse because he is drunk, he drinks in order to abuse the other members of his household, in most cases the wife.[6] This faint understanding of drinking or addiction as the root cause for domestic violence gives an advantage to the perpetrators as they would blame it on the drugs or alcohol. Often people say he is a nice chap when he is sober but when he is drunk he becomes a different person. This may be partially right but on a serious note it may just be an excuse to support that person.

c) **Misinterpretation of the Scriptures:** Domestic violence is usually seen as a private, personal and sacred relationship between the husband and the wife. It is often termed as a trial and tribulation which a good Christian wife/woman should live through as part of her Christian walk. In such circumstances she may be told to pray harder and be a better wife so that her husband may be changed. In other words, this response places the blame only on the individual. Such views are often tied up with scriptural teaching on submission.[7] For instance, the household code in Ephesians chapter 5:21-33, where wives are told to be submissive to the husband, has created an extreme reaction. Though the intent was to encourage husbands to love their wives as their own flesh, not to take them for granted but to love and respect them as part of them.[8] The understanding is that since the wife is subject to the husband he has the right to beat her. It is supposed that it is her cross which she has to bear in submission without intervention from the outside. Such misinterpretations only help in creating problem in the family especially for the woman as she is left at the mercy of her husband whether for better or for worst.

---

6 Friesen and Shamshoian, "Peacemaking in the Family: A Systematic View of Domestic Violence," 209-210.

7 H. L. Conway, *Domestic Violence and the Church*, 52.

8 Stella Baltazar, "Domestic Violence in Indian Perspective," in *Women Resisting Violence*, Eds. Mary John Mananzan, et al. (Eugene, Oregon: Wipf and Stock Publishers, 2004), 58-59.

d) **Inaction of Law Enforcement and Judicial System:** Laws are enacted so that the right of an individual is recognized and the perpetrator is punished for any action that violates rights enshrined in the law. But it does not happen in real life, in many cases the law enforcing agencies does not involve with the assumption that it is a private problem. This in turn helps promote violence as there are no actions taken. For example, section 498A of the Indian Penal Code states that if a husband or relative of the husband subjects such woman to cruelty shall be punished with imprisonment for a term which may extend to three years and shall also be liable for fine.[9] But it is sad to note that though this provision exists there is no mechanism to examine the cruelty faced by the wife/woman. The inaction of the law enforcing agencies and lack of proper mechanism to safeguard the rights of the women, domestic violence continues (Let us hope that the Domestic Violence Bill passed by the Indian Parliament in 2005 will be effective).

e) **Culture of Violence:** The theory of cultural patterning of violence holds that violence is part of our culture, part of the normal day to day life in our society. Family is a part of the culture and so violence also becomes a part of it. According to Baron and Straus, "the more a society tends to endorse the use of physical force to attain socially approved ends the greater is the likelihood...of being approved in the family and relations between sexes."[10] Domestic violence is thus a pattern of violence derived from the perpetrator constantly immersed in the culture that accepts and promotes violence. For example, a child witnesses father battering the mother on many occasions yet he goes unpunished, toys brought by the adult which is a replica of some action heroes, televisions shows and movies where certain goals are achieved through the use of force and violence. All these contribute towards the development of violent behavior in an individual and one may end up more violent and aggressive with no respect for the others.

---

9 Harneet Chima, "The Efficacy of Laws in Preventing Domestic Violence," in *Crime and Women*, ed. Ruchi Ghosh Dastidar, 208.

10 H. L. Conway, *Domestic Violence and the Church*, 63-65.

f) **Fear and Submission:** Though there are many highly educated and qualified professionals, many women continue to accept a secondary status in marriage. They feel that the onus of making the marriage work is on them. They accept that the man's career comes first and theirs is only second. Children's future is far more important than their own suffering. Many wife/women facing domestic violence tolerate the intolerable as long as they can. They hope that things will get better. They are afraid that if things fall apart they will be blamed.[11]

In a survey conducted among the victims of domestic violence it was found that the fear of social and religious stigma and shame leads to further violence. If a wife is asked why she does not opt for divorce, there is the fear of blame from families, friends and society. Why the matter is not reported to the law enforcing agencies, the fear is they will do nothing and if the husband comes to know of it, it will create further problems. Children facing violence at homes also had the same feelings to share. They say what if they are driven out of home? What if their parents get arrested? What if their friends stop mingling with them? All these fears prevent them to approach the law enforcing agencies involved in protecting them.

5. Effects of Domestic Violence

a) On the wife/women: Although both husbands and wives or men and women can be abused and can be victims of violence, in most cases it is the wives/women who had to suffer the most. L. Walker in her study of the effects of domestic violence found out that wife/women suffering violence at home had the following syndrome:

i. Low self-esteem.
ii. Accepted responsibility for the batterer's action.
iii. Suffered from guilt yet denied the anger and terror they felt.
iv. Presented a passive face to the world.
v. Had severe stress reactions with psycho-physiological complaints.
vi. Had traditional views about home and family.

11 Suseela Mathew, *Breaking the Barriers* (Bangalore: Christian Institute for the Study of Religion and Society, n. d. cited as S. Mathew, *Breaking the Barriers*, 31.

vii. Believed that no one could resolve the predicament except themselves.[12]

b) On the Adolescents: Adolescence is a particularly stressful stage and that stress becomes more acute for teenagers from violent homes. The effect can be such that it can lead to drug and alcohol abuse which they will see as an only option to escape from these problems. There is also every possibility that they will run away from home leading to a strained relation with the family members. It can also lead to suicidal tendencies, homicidal thoughts and actions.[13]

c) On the Children: Domestic violence destroys the safe environment in which children should ideally grow and develop their personality and positive characters. The messages of love and protection which give them emotional stability are shattered because the parents, who are their primary source of physical nourishment and emotional stability are engaged in bewildering exchanges of violence. Global studies show that children who have witnessed violence in the home, whether they are directly assaulted or not are at higher risk to become the next generation of abusers. They are also on the way to develop chronic or serious illness, physical disability or limited cognitive development. It can also lead to post traumatic stress disorder (PTSD) and depression. A child may become confused, insecure, and often assume violence as a norm and life style. Children who see their mothers being victimized are five times more likely to exhibit serious behavioral problems than other children. They are six times more likely to commit suicide, twenty four times more likely to commit sexual assault, fifty percent more likely to abuse drug and alcohol and seventy four percent more likely to commit crimes against others.[14]

6. Some Remedial Measures

a) No human being needs to bear this kind of suffering. Awareness programs and the necessity of making victims get help and access to help and intervention at an initial stage should be stressed.

---

12 H. L. Conway, *Domestic Violence and the Church*, 19-20.

13 Ibid., 32-33.

14 Friesen & Shamshoian, "Peacemaking in the Family," 214-215.

b) Engage agencies and organizations to intervene whenever such violations of human rights take place.

c) Legislation alone cannot help in bringing change required; there is a need for commitment of people from social, political, and religious spheres to create a culture where acts of domestic violence become totally unacceptable.

d) Victims especially wives/women need to be encouraged to express their own views and create solidarity networks.

e) Wives/Women need to be empowered and informed so that they are aware of their legal rights, and can support each other. Let them join hands with insightful men and women in building a vibrant and healthy community.[15]

f) Public awareness campaigns like slogans and images for pamphlets, fliers, posters, and TV or radio spots on domestic violence.

g) Engage Development agencies and charitable trusts to join hands with human right advocates by providing financial support to domestic violence activism.[16]

Conclusion

In conclusion, I would like to state that domestic violence continues to exist within families in one way or the other. It is not only an insignificant difficulty faced by a small minority but a widespread phenomenon. As human being we are very much part and parcel of the society, if it is not checked today it may led to further violence and may hamper the growth and development of the society. Domestic violence has been affecting the lives of individuals in the family both physically and mentally. In such circumstances, the duty for us may not to take it as part of the norm nor a private affair where we cannot interfere, we have every right to involve ourselves. We need to see to it that proper legal measures are framed and enforced, the rights of the victims recognized and protected, then only one can combat this systematic of violence. The church as a voice of the voiceless need to speak for the rights of the victims, and seek measures to put a stop

15 S. Mathew, *Breaking the Barriers,* 30-32.

16 Janet Elise Johnson, *Gender Violence in Russia* (Bloomington, Indiana: Indiana University Press, 2009), 93.

to such atrocities. It cannot remain a mere spectator when innocent are victimized and threatened. Violence begets violence, thus a non-violent intervention is the need of the hour. I would like to end with a poem from Taslima Nasrin, the Bangladeshi poet, titled "At the Back of Progress."

> The fellow who sits in the air-conditioned office
> Is the one who in his youth raped
> A dozen or so young girls,
> And, at cocktail parties, is secretly stricken with lust,
> Fastening his eyes on lovelies' bellybuttons.
> In five-star hotels,
> He tries out his different sexual tastes
> With a variety of women,
> Then returns home and beats his wife
> Because of an over-ironed handkerchief or shirt collar.
> In his office Mr. Big puffs on a cigarette,
> Shuffles through files
> Rings for his employees, shouts, demands tea, drinks,
> And return to writing people's character references.
> His employee speaks in such a low voice
> That no one would ever suspect
> How, at home, he also raises his voice, is vile to his family
> But with his buddies on the porch or at a movie
> Indulge in loud harangues on politics, art literature, and how some female-
> His mother, grandmother or great grandmother-committed suicide
> Bidding goodbye to his buddies, he returns home,
> Over a bar of soap or the baby's pneumonia
> Next day, at work, he pleasantly brings the tea,
> Keeps the lighter in his pocket,
> Receives a tip of a couple of taka,
> And tells no one that he divorced his first wife for her sterility,
> His second for giving birth to a daughter,
> His third for not brining a sufficient dowry.
> Now, with wife number four, he again has someone:
> To beat over a green chili or a handful of rice.[17]

17 Taslima Nasrin, "At the Back of Progress," in *Musings on Vital Issues,* edited by P. J. George (Chennai: Orient Blackswan Private Limited, 2010), 116-117.

5

Patriarchy and Domestic Violence

Toshimenla Jamir[1]

Introduction

In most societies, there are significant differences and inequalities between women and men in responsibilities assigned, activities undertaken, access to and control over resources, as well as decision-making opportunities. Throughout human civilization, women's status is primarily viewed through the prism of their reproductive and nurturant role, which was further legitimated over the ages through customs and legislations. This process has effectively restricted their mobility in the social and political space. The socio-cultural system that systematically excluded women from the mainstream, keeping them less capable and denying them equal opportunities is shaped and strengthened by the values embodied in patriarchy. Patriarchy is understood as "a system of social structures and practices in which men dominate, oppress and exploit women" (Perron 1995). Patriarchy is both a system and ideology. Basically it holds that women's lives are governed by a concept of power that controls and subordinate women, their rights, behavior pattern, physical movements, thinking process, etc. At times, it is expressed and cultivated through customary practices and traditions, social

1 Dr. Toshimenla Jamir is Associate Professor, Department of Sociology, Nagaland University, Lumami.

norms, historical evolution, socialization process, social expectations and control over individual aspirations.

Very often patriarchal control is perpetuated through open regulations and violence. The present chapter seeks to dwell on the interface of patriarchy and domestic violence in its various dimensions.

1. Patriarchy: An Exposition

Patriarchy literally means "the rule of the father" and comes from the Greek (*patriarkhēs*), "father of a race" or "chief of a race, patriarch", which is a compound of (*patria*), "lineage, descent" (from *patēr*, "father") and (*arkhō*), "I rule".

Patriarchy is a social system in which maleshold primary power; they predominate in roles of political leadership, moral authority, social privilege and control of property; and, in the domain of the family, fathers or father-figures hold authority over women and children. It implies the institutions of male domination and entails female subordination. Many patriarchal societies are also patrilineal, meaning that property and title are inherited by the male lineage. Historically, the term patriarchy was used to refer to autocratic rule by the male head of a family. However, in modern times, it more generally refers to social systems in which power is primarily held by adult men. Anthropological evidence suggests that most prehistoric hunter-gatherer societies were relatively egalitarian, and that patriarchal social structures did not develop until many years after the end of the Pleistocene era, following social and technological innovations such as agriculture and domestication. According to Robert M. Strozier, historical research has not yet found a specific "initiating event". Some scholars point to about six thousand years ago (4000 BCE), when the concept of fatherhood took root, as the beginning of the spread of patriarchy.

However, James DeMeo argues that a specific initiating event does exist - the geographical record shows that climate change around 4000 BCE led to famines in the Sahara, Arabian peninsula and what are now the Central Asian deserts which then resulted in the adoption of warlike, patriarchal structures in order to secure food sources:

> *Famine, starvation and mass-migrations related to land-abandonment severely traumatised the originally peaceful and sex-positive inhabitants of those lands, inducing a distinct turning away from original matrism towards patristic forms of behavior.*

Domination by men of women is found in the Ancient Near East as far back as 3100 BCE, as are restrictions on a woman's reproductive capacity and exclusion from "the process of representing or the construction of history". With the appearance of the Hebrews, there is also "the exclusion of woman from the God-humanity covenant".

A prominent Greek general Meno, in the Platonic dialogue of the same name, sums up the prevailing sentiment in Classical Greece about the respective virtues of men and women. He says:

> Let us take first the virtue of a man—he should know how to administer the state, and in the administration of it to benefit his friends and harm his enemies; and he must also be careful not to suffer harm himself. *A woman's virtue, if you wish to know about that, may also be easily described: her duty is to order her house, and keep what is indoors, and obey her husband.*

The works of Aristotle portrayed women as morally, intellectually, and physically inferior to men. He saw women as the property of men and claimed that women's role in society was to reproduce and serve men in the household; and saw male domination of women as natural and virtuous. Gerda Lerner (1986), in the book *The Creation of Patriarchy*, states that Aristotle believed that women had colder blood than men, which made women not evolve into men, the sex that Aristotle believed to be perfect and superior. Maryanne Cline Horowotz stated that Aristotle believed that "soul contributes the form and model of creation." This implies that any imperfection that is caused in the world must be caused by a woman because one cannot acquire an imperfection from perfection (which he perceived as male). Aristotle had a hierarchical ruling structure in his theories. Gerda Lerner claims that through this patriarchal belief system, passed down generation to generation, people have been conditioned to believe that men are superior to women. These symbols are benchmarks which children learn about when they grow up, and the cycle of patriarchy continues much past the Greeks.

From around the 19th Century, many women actively began to question the commonly accepted patriarchal interpretation of Christian scripture. One of the foremost of these was Sarah Grimké, who voiced skepticism about the ability of men to translate and interpret passages relating to the roles of the sexes without bias. She proposed alternative translations and interpretations of passages relating to women, and she applied historical and cultural criticism to a number of verses, arguing that their admonitions applied to specific historical situations, and were not to be viewed as universal commands. Elizabeth Cady Stanton used Grimké's criticism of biblical sources to establish a basis for feminist thought. She published *The Woman's Bible*, which proposed a feminist reading of the Old and New Testament. This tendency was enlarged by feminist theory, which denounced the patriarchal Judeo-Christian tradition.

In contemporary academic discourse, there is an ongoing debate between biological and sociological explanations of the phenomenon of patriarchy. As a common standard of differentiation between genders, advocates for a patriarchal society like to focus on the influences that hormones have over biological systems. Hormones have been declared as the 'key to the sexual universe' because they are present in all animals and are the driving force in two critical developmental stages - sex-determinism in the fetus, and puberty in the teenage individual. Playing a critical role in the development of the brain and behavior, testosterone and estrogen have been labeled the 'male-hormone' and 'female-hormone' respectively as a result of the impact they have when masculinizing or feminizing an individual.

Most sociologists predominantly reject biological explanations of patriarchy and contend that social and cultural conditionings are primarily responsible for establishing male and female gender roles. According to standard sociological theory, patriarchy is the result of sociological constructions that are passed down from generation to generation. These constructions are most pronounced in societies with traditional cultures and less economic development. The idea that patriarchy is natural has come under attack from many sociologists who argue that patriarchy evolved due to historical, rather than biological, conditions. In technologically simple societies, men's greater physical strength and women's common experience of pregnancy combined together to sustain patriarchy. In whatever form patriarchy may be expressed, gender studies perspective holds the view that in the ultimate analysis, patriarchy is a form of violence against women as it suppresses women's rights and achievement, and denies justice and equality.

2. Gender-Based Violence

One of the most obvious manifestations of the unequal status of men and women and perception of their inferior status based on patriarchal ideology can be seen in the widespread perpetration of violence against women. Studies over recent years indicate that perpetration of gross forms of violence against women, whether through state agencies, in the community, or in the family, is a manifestation of women's unequal status and perception of their inferior status in the family and community. International bodies such as the United Nations (UN) today regard violence against women as the most pervasive yet least recognized human rights abuse in the world which jeopardizes women's lives, bodies, psychological integrity and freedom. Accordingly, the Vienna Human Rights Conference and the Fourth World Conference on Women gave priority to this issue. The UN Convention on the Elimination of all forms of Discrimination against Women (CEDAW) defined gender-based violence as any act of violence that results in, or is likely to result in physical, sexual or psychological harm or suffering to women, including threats to such acts, coercion or arbitrary deprivations to liberty, whether occurring in public or private life. The concept encompasses a wide range of violations, including sexual abuse of women and children, rape, sexual harassment, trafficking of women and girls, female infanticide or foeticide, harmful traditional practices such as Female Genital Mutilation (FGM), dowry related violence, the Devadesi system (wherein young girls from low caste communities are dedicated to a god or goddess and exploited in prostitution), and domestic violence. Gender-based violence both reflects and reinforces inequities between men and women and compromises the health, dignity, security and autonomy of its victims. Any one of these abuses can leave deep psychological scars, damage the health of women and girls in general, including their reproductive and sexual health, and in some instances, results in death.

"Violence against women both violates and impairs or nullifies the enjoyment by women of their human rights and fundamental freedoms... In all societies, to a greater or lesser degree, women and girls are subjected to physical, sexual and psychological abuse that cuts across lines of income, class and culture" (*Beijing Declaration and Platform for Action, paragraph 112).*

3. Domestic Violence

One form of gender-based violence that cuts across class, ethnicity, race or cultural differences is domestic violence. The World Health Organization's (WHO) World Report on Violence and Health notes that 'one of the most common forms of violence against women is that performed by a husband or male partner'. The Indian protection of women from Domestic Violence Act 2005 defines domestic violence as an act, omission, commission or conduct that leads to physical, verbal, emotional, sexual and financial abuse; or, an act or omission that huts or degrades a woman by the husband/male partner, relative and other family members who are living together in a common space or shared household. This type of violence is frequently invisible since it happens behind closed doors, and effectively, when legal systems and cultural norms do not treat as a crime, but rather as a 'private' family matter, or a normal part of life. Most domestic violence involves male anger directed against women partners.

Domestic violence may be correlated to many sociological factors which are underpinned by patriarchal ideologies ranging from women's subordinated status in society to the deprivation of property rights in most cultures. UN data shows that women, who comprise approximately half of the world's population, own only one percent of the world's property and resources. This is indicative of the dispossessed status of women around the world. The consequence is the economic dependence of many women on their male relatives, including husbands for their sustenance. It renders many women vulnerable to domestic violence and abuses at the hands of their male partners. Abused women tend to tolerate the violence against them as most do not see other options open to them.

A recent study (Panda & Agarwal, 2005) point out that enhanced property status can render women less vulnerable to domestic violence. In the cited study, 49 percent of respondents (women) without property reported physical violence and 84 percent reported psychological violence. However, among respondents with land and a house, only 7 per cent reported physical violence and 16 per cent reported psychological violence. Very significantly, 71 percent of propertied women who suffered domestic violence left their husbands as compared to only 19 per cent of property-less women who left their husbands on account of violence. This research very clearly highlights the fact that that property and land rights can strengthen a women's fallback position and her bargaining power within marriage, which likely serves to deter domestic violence. And because these rights can enhance a women's self-worth, they can thereby reduce her tolerance to violence. Hence, laws of inheritance, which very often is determined by patriarchal values, do indirectly perpetuate the phenomenon of domestic violence in many societies. This brings into focus the imperative of re-assessing the Personal and Customary laws of many communities which tend to marginalize women and girls from property rights.

The patriarchal notion of males as the undisputed head of the family does also play a role in perpetuating domestic violence. It is an accepted notion in many traditional cultures that the head of the family wields ultimate authority over the wife and children, who has the prerogative to take all major decisions in the household. Instances of wife battering by the husband are often lightly glossed over as 'disciplining' the wife which should be regarded as their private affair. Such attitude serves to encourage the abusive husbands to continue subjugating their wives. Most often than not, the victims maintain a stoic silence for fear of social stigma, not only for herself, but for her children as well.

Cases of domestic violence are not confined to the uneducated or economically disadvantaged section of society. It is prevalent even amongst highly educated professional families where both spouses are earning members. Therefore, it is a social phenomenon that cuts across all sections of society driven by the values of patriarchy.

4. Seeking Ways to End the Violence

Gender-based violence serves to perpetuate male power and control. It is sustained by a culture of silence and denial of the seriousness of the health consequences of abuse. In addition, to the harm they exact on the individual level, these consequences also exact a social toll and place a heavy and unnecessary burden on health services.Violence against women is inextricably linked to gender-based inequalities when women and girls are expected to be generally subservient. The important challenge that confronts us is whether gender-based violence is inevitable or is it possible to arrive at ways and means to overcome this phenomenal social problem. One overarching issue that cannot be avoided is the question of whether domestic and other forms of gender based violence are biologically or socially determined. Cross-cultural studies have found that nearly a fifth of peasant and small-scale societies are essentially free of domestic violence. The very existence of such cultures shows that male violence against women is not the inevitable result of male biology or sexuality, but more a matter of how society views masculinity. Since most domestic violence involves male anger directed against their female partners and not vice-versa, this gender difference appears rooted in the way boys and men are socialized – biological factors do not seem to account for the dramatic differences in behavior in this regard between men and women.

The prevalence of domestic violence in a given society appears more as a result of tacit acceptance by that society of men's domination of women. It is determined by the way in which men themselves as men, and by the way they view women which would be to a large extent shaped by the patriarchal values of a given society. Viewed in this manner, ending violence against women would entail changing cultural concepts about masculinity. It requires a change in the paradigm of masculinity that allows for the resolution of conflict through violence. A very important strategy to be adopted in this process would be to engage men – whether they are young or old, parents, policy makers.

Though social legislation exists in the country in the form of the Protection of Women from Domestic Violence Act 2005, many women still lack awareness regarding the legal provisions of the Act. The fact that under the said Act, each district across the country should appoint Protection Officers for victims of domestic violence is not known to most women the author of this article interacted with.

Notwithstanding the provisions of the law under which victims may take recourse in cases of domestic violence, the most important thing is to change traditional attitude of male superiority and female subordination. This necessitates a reassessment of deep seated patriarchal attitudes entrenched in various institutions and norms that allow for the perpetuation of male domination over their female counterparts. The key is to arrive at an equation where men and women can walk together on an equal pace as partners in family and society based on the universally accepted ideal of gender equality.

6

Politics of Tribal Customary Practices Vis-a-Vis Silencing the Victims of Domestic Violence

L. Imsutoshi Jamir[1]

> *Many people who wish to impose their definition of reality would deny that they are involved in gaining power. They would say that because of their greater knowledge, wisdom, training and experience they know what is best. The most dangerous people in the world are those who believe that they know what is best for others* – **Masson**

I want to pose few questions as I discuss my personal observation on domestic violence at the backdrop of customary practices. If male-on-female violence was a part of tribal culture? Or if domestic violence was very much prevailing in tribal communities? Or if discussion on domestic violence in the context of tribal customary practices can be justified? These queries may demand our broad understanding of what is domestic violence in order to provide our response to the questions posed. At the same time, closer look at the domestic violence in tribal communities may suggest that the issue is also linked to gender issue.

In most cases, the perpetrators of domestic violence in tribal communities were/are most often described as men who were grandfathers, fathers, step-fathers and were also often accepted by

1 Dr. L. Imsutoshi Jamir is Associate Professor, Department of Communication and Director of CCCRC the Clark Theological College, Aolijen.

community as being important people within the community. And often these elders consciously exploit the most backward elements of traditional culture to justify their action. As such, conspicuously, in most cases, men's supposedly 'customary right' to abuse their women and children, may be the main factor that contributes towards domestic violence in tribal families.

Living in a culture of violence,[2] I would like to argue that domestic violence is reinforced by cultural values and beliefs that are repeatedly communicated through societal institutions and other customary practices and beliefs that tolerate it. The perpetrator's violence is further supported when peers, family members, or others in the community minimize or ignore the abuse and fail to provide consequences. As a result, the abuser learns that not only is the behavior justified, but also it is acceptable.

1. Understanding Domestic Violence in Tribal Communities

Comparatively late comer, yet the present tribal society is marked by the breaking of silence about the prevalence and impact of domestic violence. This period can be characterised as one in which the community is confronted by new ways of analysing violence against humanity particularly violence against women and children at home. Both academia as well as society in general are involved in this human right activity with commitment or at least as a matter of luxury. This, I think is due to the unprecedented occurrences of domestic violence in our present context as well as people's consciousness about the human rights endowed to every person.

However, the recent years also have seen challenges to established views of violence, and have been marked by attempts to silence victims and survivors again, and also to discredit those who believe their stories and advocate on their behalf. A notable example in the tribal society is the unreasonable and unscientific acceptance of (some) the tribal customary practices and beliefs that victimises, particularly women and children in tribal societies. I sincerely think that these challenges have demonstrated the need for research-based intervention with an aim to develop innovative practices designed to meet the emergent challenges.

2 E.g., violent movies or videogames, community norms, and cultural beliefs.

Domestic violence is a pattern of coercive and assaultive behaviors that include physical, sexual, verbal, and psychological attacks and economic coercion that adults or adolescents use against their intimate partner. It is the pervasive and methodical use of threats, intimidation, manipulation, and physical violence by someone who seeks power and control over their intimate partner. In most cases, domestic violence has been framed and understood exclusively as a women's issue and that women are the victims of domestic violence. But, men also can be victims of abuse, children may not only experience domestic violence but are also affected by exposure to domestic violence. To look from broader angle, domestic violence cuts across every segment of society and occurs in all age, racial, ethnic, socio-economic, sexual orientation, and religious groups. Domestic violence is a social, economic, cultural, religious and health concern.

The prevailing context and nature of domestic violence in tribal society are more typically organized and therefore the effects of domestic violence on victims are more naturally accepted and experienced by the victims. For instance, Rosemary Hunter from her research on the experience of women[3] who attempt redress against violence and harassment by family members or work colleagues argues that the emphasis on 'consent'[4] or 'compromise' results in a lack of institutional affirmation of women's stories of abuse. Thus, the existence of violence against women, children, disabled, etc., and the scale of that violence, fails to enter the realm of public knowledge. May be, denial and minimisation of violence at home at the pretext of established practice and beliefs is one of the major reasons why the seriousness of domestic violence is not occupying public discussion.

In tribal society, victims of domestic violence do not possess a set of common or universal characteristics or personality character,

---

3 Rosemary Hunter, "Having Her Day in Court? Violence, Legal Remedies and Consent", in *Innovative Responses to Sexual and Domestic Violence* (pp. 59-68), edited by Jan Breckenridge and Lesley Laing. St Leonards NSW, Australia: Allen & Unwin, 1999.

4 Mutually agreed settlements. In our context this mutually agreed settlements are the outcome of long and cherished customary or traditional practices and believe which demands unconditional acceptance of the hegemonic practice.

but they do share the common experience of being abused by someone close to them.[5] Normally, victims of domestic violence in tribal societies are not easily recognized because, may be they are not usually covered in marks or bruises. If there are injuries, victims have often learned to conceal them to avoid detection, suspicion, and *shame*.[6] May be the victims, often women and children in tribal society consider such violence only as normal everyday occurrence and society as well look at it the same way. Unfortunately, an array of misconceptions about victims of domestic violence in tribal society has led to harmful stereotypes and myths about who they are and the realities of their abuse. Victims may not feel stigmatization and community too may misunderstand by looking at it as normal everyday life in tribal family.[7] At the same time, perpetrators of domestic violence in tribal societies may be well-intended family members.[8] The common myths such as, 'only poor, uneducated women, disobedient children, or irresponsible wife who undermine domestic responsibilities are victims of domestic violence', or 'victims usually provoke and therefore deserve the violence they experience', or myth such as 'men, parents, elders has the 'given' (sole) authority and responsibility to 'control', or 'unquestionable submission to men, elders and parents by wife, children and younger ones'. These unquestionable myths legitimise domestic violence in tribal society.

5 Anyone can become a victim of domestic violence. Victims of domestic violence can be women, men, adolescents, disabled persons, children and can be of any age.

6 There is always trepidation of 'what my neighbor will say', 'what my children will say', 'what my friends will say' in the minds of the victims. On the one hand there is misconception of 'disobedience vis-à-vis punishment as the causes of domestic violence' and on the other hand, stereotyping family and what happens in the family as private affairs and is beyond the boundary of community's responsibility.

7 In most of the tribal family tradition, children are to show unconditional obedience to their parents. Sometimes, respect and obedience to elders, parents is being misused. Often, father as the head of the family is being used as benefit to abuse, control and dominate wife and children.

8 They may be 'responsible parents', 'loving brother or sister' who exercises power 'over' wife, children or younger brother or sister at the pretext of being 'responsible'.

At the same time closer look at these myths may suggest a clear indication that they steamed from ideology of tribal customary practices.

2. Customary Practices and Politics of Differences

Identity and meaning are based on difference. Visual images, signs and meaning are result of difference. And the process of differentiating is endless.[9] For instance, in order to understand the term 'tribal man' we need more terms like 'tribal woman', 'Indian men', 'Indian women', etc. By this I mean to recognise differences between 'men and women', or 'children and parents' or 'owner and servant' (master-slave) as a starting point. We need to examine 'how our very notions of identity and difference are grounded in historical, political, cultural and moral relations. However, there is a politics of difference in tribal communities. There is 'issue' of those who are marked as 'different' whilst a notion of 'us' and 'them' persists. Until we are able to sincerely and consciously acknowledge that 'we are all "culturally different" rather than "we are normal" and "they are different" and unless we are able to acknowledge the need of 'mutual acceptance' and 'mutual respect' on the basis of 'equals' and unless we involve in the dialogue between our differences without baggage of male hegemonic attitudes or superior 'us' against inferior 'them' or 'stronger us' against 'weaker them' we certainly will not establish a meaningful dialogue between our differences and will not be in any way possible to overcome domestic violence prevailing in our tribal homes'.

3. Customary Practices and the Politics of Power

Central to the politics of differences or any theoretical frameworks we formulate, will suggest the importance of acknowledging the issue of 'power' that interplay.[10] Both feminist and narrative frameworks are built on understanding the impact of power, particularly as enacted

---

9 See also Post-structuralism study. For poststructuralism language is never stable.

10 For more information on relationship between power and knowledge, see the works of Michel Foucault, *Power/Knowledge: Selected Interviews and Other Writings,* edited by Colin Gardon (New York: Pantheon, 1980).

in relationships and society generally. Power and knowledge are linked. People who posses power employ knowledge to discriminate and marginalized those lack power. This marginalization is rendered natural through a system of commonly circulated beliefs called ideology. For instance, a feminist analysis clearly articulates issues of power in relation to gender. It identifies women's inequality within society and identifies the structures and processes that seek to maintain this. Our understanding of a feminist approach to 'domestic violence' or 'victims of domestic violence' is often demarcated within a socio-economic, decision making, male hegemonic political context. It may not be wrong to identify 'traditional customary practices' that facilitates an understanding of the broad range of relationships between male and female and ways women are expected to socialise, interact, associate and resist.

In the context of domestic violence, it is important to challenge traditional customary practices that provides undue hegemonic power and control to men over women and children. I said this, because in most cases, the upholders of such practices have the notion that 'customary practices' are the key in maintaining the harmonious co-existence among tribals throughout the existence of tribal society without giving much consciousness of how such belief and practices victimizes the 'others'. The notion of the 'elders' (men) as 'expert'[11] need to be challenged. Instead, we need to develop a theoretical orientations, where woman (victims) are seen as the expert in relation to their own life experiences. Men, elders, parents, owners as 'experienced', may have expertise, experience, knowledge and resources to support and assist the 'others', but must not take the position of the 'expert' on a person's life. We believe that the expert does not know more than the victims about their experience, rather the victims are the expert on themselves.

11 'Expert' is underlined in relation to *knowledge*- 'authority' and 'sole custodian' of traditional customary practices in determining how family and society should function, how such practices should uphold, interpret, execute and follow.

4. Customary Practices and Politics of Universal Values

The tribal customary law or practices which (in most cases) are ethical in nature are related to individual and societal behaviour. Many tribal communities believe that the tribal customary law and practices are associated with their origin and development as social community. Some even claimed that in the beginning their ancestors were living together with God who taught them the codes and norms. These laws were transmitted orally from one generation to another. Moreover, these customs and laws were considered to consist of truth. People presumes that such customs and practices provide justice and has a public utility and therefore community observed it as moral, religious and social codes. Violation of such practices is strictly considered as against God and against the harmonious co-existence of the community and family. In the present situation, customary law and practices of tribal communities are labelled as having universal values that cannot be challenged, contested and argued upon. In most cases, though women and children are victimised and denied their rights, such undesired practices are left unchallenged and unquestioned.

I would like to argue that, no matter how beautiful and elaborate such laws and practices may be, they are human construction in the course of historical situation. Moreover, closer look at such practices may even suggest the interplay of power and politics. Thus, deconstructing traditional practices may be necessary in order to construct tribal customary practices and beliefs to overcome domestic violence.

5. Customary Practices and Politics of Subjugation

Subjugation refers to processes that subordinate or discount certain types of experiences or sources of information, by either ignoring or reinterpreting the content. In relation to domestic or sexual violence in tribal society, subjugation occurs when elders (men) 'knowledge', and their ways of talking about violence (discourses), are privileged over the knowledge that victims hold about their own experiences. The politics of subjugation provides an understanding of how elders asserts, "they know what is best for others' and how the marginalisation of the voice of the victim of domestic violence necessarily complemented the privileging of tribal customary practices and believes of the elders.

It was customary to talk about such as lack of housing and poverty. These were the issues that were publicly spoken about and which became the community's concern. Consequently, the protection of women and children was awarded little value and the victim's own knowledge and experience of abuse effectively remained invisible. Thus, a culturally induced shame of admitting to being a victim of violence in the home privatised and subjugated the issues of sexual and domestic violence. Everything worked together- family members, elders, and community- to subjugate the experiences of those who suffered domestic violence. Individual, systemic, and societal barriers faced by victims of domestic violence includes, fear, helplessness, isolation, guilt and shame, emotional and physical impairment, individual belief system, cultural hurdles. All these are associated with politics of subjugation. Moreover, the politics of subjugation provides an equally important means of understanding how statistics, report and documentation of domestic violence has been disguised or masked. Thus, politics of subjugation in tribal communities has a very serious impact both in the lives of the victims as well as the oppressors and general public.

6. Customary Practices and Politics of Silencing

Subjugation is only one part of a dual system that facilitates a context in which victims struggle to speak of their experiences in the public domain. Victims' experiences of sexual and domestic violence are subjugated alongside the operation of 'silences' within tribal customary discourses. Silences refer to 'the things one declines to say, or is forbidden to name. Silences, then, have been an equally effective technique operating to omit or mask different aspects of a narrative, thereby changing its meaning and significance. Silences have had a very particular and dramatic effect on the victim of domestic violence and are evidenced in two ways. First, silences are apparent in ways of speaking about domestic violence. For instance, child physical abuse may be explained and interpreted as 'neglect' of the parents. The effect of such generalised discussion is that it hides the different gendered dynamics and any specific effects it may have on its victims, thereby making child sexual assault invisible.

The second way in which silences may be incorporated in tribal customary discourses encompasses speaking about domestic and sexual assault, but in mythologised ways that effectively silence a particular voice, that of the victim. The concept of 'mythology' is intended to portray the process by which explanations of events are interpretations imposed from above, rather than constructions that reflect the experiences of the victims from the bottom up. For example, after the perpetrator of a rape had pleaded guilty for his act, the village elders alleged that if the woman 'had been doing the right thing she would not have been raped'. The most insidious aspect of such mythology is that very often victims internalise these beliefs and therefore struggle to make sense of their experiences, let alone speak of them publicly. In this situation, victims such as children and women were disqualified from speaking of their experiences so their stories remained unheard. Victim's ability to tell the truth is suppressed by often blaming the victim and obscuring the responsibility of the perpetrator affects those victims who have experienced domestic violence.

7. Customary Practices and Politics of Superior Detachment

Human beings can give an account of themselves and of their place in the world. What a culture would be where no one any longer knew what it meant to narrate things'. Treating people as if they lack that capacity is to treat them as if they were not human. Yet, as tribal communities, we have grown used to ways of organizing things that ignore voice, that assume voice does not matter. The past century provides many shameful examples of just this. The tribal traditions have many derogatory images and sayings about women and interestingly people still believe in them and therefore dispense women only with stereotyped role in the private sphere and made them voiceless. For instance, some tribal sayings include, 'women and crabs have no religion', 'a wife and a broken fence can be easily changed', 'a women's wisdom does not cross the village brook', 'the words of women and the horns of the female mithun are of no use', 'the speaking of women is like the chirping of birds at night'. In this context, R. L. Hnuni observed, "Today these expressions are still known, though they tend to be used playfully. But the ideology of women's inferiority embodied in the sayings is difficult to put away completely."[12]

Such believes have penetrated in the structures and customary practices of tribal society. Not forgetting its role in the socialization process by describing the roles and duties of both women and men. This problematic has its affect on two fronts. First, these sayings and images have perceptibly influenced men to have negative attitude towards women. Second, significantly, these images leave a deep imprint upon women's self perception. Narola Imchen argues, "one of the consequences of the patriarchal culture is that it not only convinces men that women are inferior but also convinces women themselves that they are inferior.[13] Such beliefs and practices undermine women's experiences, wisdom and capabilities and further establish detachment between male superiority and women inferiority. This is what I call politics of male superior detachment. Unfortunately, vast mute majorities-victims-have yielded their potential rights in the name of such traditional practices demanding practically nothing in exchange. At the same time, the politics of male superior detachment have established myth of isolated mind and reinforces what I call, 'formal procedure of justice'.[14]

8. Concluding Remarks

The contributor has presented this research work with much fear and trepidation. He is afraid that his approach to tribal customary practices might be labelled as against tribal identity and ethos and may even consider as 'enemy' to the current euphoric about revitalization of tribal tradition and practices. However, as discussed

---

12 R. L. Hnuni, "Vision for Women in North East India", in *Transforming Theology for Empowering Women: A Theological and Hermeneutical Reflection in the context of North East India,* edited by R. L. Hnuni (Jorhat: Women Study Centre, Eastern Theological College, 1999), 146.

13 Narola Imchen, *Women in Church and Society: The Story of Ao Naga Women* (Jorhat: Eastern Theological College, 2001), 13. Cf. L. Imsutoshi Jamir, "Globalization of Culture: Challenges for Doing Theology in Asia", *The Journal of Theologies and Cultures in Asia,* 2, 2003, 167-182.

14 For more detail discussion, see my article "Moality of Inter-subjectivity: Toward Inclusive Tribal Community", *Journal of Tribal Studies,* Vol. XVI, No. 2, 2011, 16-31.

in the preceding pages, the concern of this research is to give expression to caution. What we need is to have an existentially objective understanding of tribal customary practices even at the cost of deconstructing some of the customary practices with an aim to overcome domestic violence prevalent in our present context.

Customary law in tribal society requires being critically evaluated and transformed into a jurisprudence that is relevant and consistent with the values and principles acceptable to all the section of people. Moreover, it is also imperative that the existing tribal customary law remains founded on values, a jurisprudence, that is relevant to all-encompassing tribal life.[15] In other words, we must be able to take from our (past) traditions - all that is good, just, inclusive so as to give a new dimension to our culture. At the same time, tribal customary laws need not became only as 'monumental' by referring it only when manipulation becomes necessary. Through this process, tribals would have the opportunity to address their perspective of laws, conduct and institutions within a new comprehensive ethical framework of restorative justice that includes democracy, equality, respect and dignity of all.

Bearing in mind the 'community' nature of tribal society and on which tribal theology is founded, the importance of customary law that governed and maintained tribal community/ies cannot be negated. At the same time, it is equally important for customary law to be based on a jurisprudence that affirms life and dignity of all, irrespective of gender and age. Once the process for tribal jurisprudence has evolved, the prevailing sides that undermine 'justice to and for all', 'equal participation of all in decision making process', and most importantly inconsistencies in the present customary law and practices can be addressed both at the functional, as well as the conceptual levels. This is another risky but unavoidable terrain where tribal scholars must venture in for the purpose of doing tribal theology with boldness and clarity. Developing innovative approach that encompasses dignity, justice equality and respect to 'all' could be a pathfinder, and capable of addressing the debate associated with 'right and truth'.

---

15 I think tribals need to be able to take what is good from the past and transform this knowledge into the present day relevance.

7

Customary Law/Judiciary and Domestic Violence in Naga Context

Atungo Shitri[1]

Crimes against women encompasses a wide range of human rights violations, including sexual abuse of girl child, rape, domestic violence, sexual harassment, abduction, trafficking of women and girls and several gender biased traditional practices.

Statistics from National Crime Records Bureau's (NCRB) Crime in India 2012 report reveals that Nagaland had the lowest rate of crime against women in the region - 1.9 per cent. The NCRB registered only 38 cases of crime against women in 2011 in Nagaland. However, there should be no room for complacency because the data itself may be misleading since not all crimes are reported and registered for several reasons. Hence, one must not assume that the state is safe for women because every now and then shocking stories of rape, sexual assault, child molestation, abduction, etc., is taking place rampantly.

The root cause of violence and crimes against women in Nagaland perhaps is attributed directly or indirectly to our customary practices. We have patriarchal family system where male is the dominant head of the family. Even within a family itself, gender disparity is systematically practiced and is emphasized by

1 Mr. Atungo Shitri is currently the Secretary, Peace & Justice Ministries, CBCNEI, Guwahati.

traditional norms. Female members are expected to serve male in subdued manner, and should not rebel against his command. Women rights are disparaged in decision making, in voicing out opinion or inheriting property.

It may be pertinent to mention here that in the Northeast region, women enjoy greater mobility and visibility comparatively with women from other parts of the country. Practices such as dowry related violence or bride burning is not very prevalent in the region. This may be often cited to portray a picture of equity between men and women in the region and has given rise to the presumption that violence against women is not a major concern in the area. Data collected by the North East Network, however, suggests that violence against women, particularly domestic violence, is on the rise in the Northeast.

Violence against women is a manifestation of the historically unequal power relations between men and women, which have led to domination over and discrimination against women by men and to the prevention of women's full advancement (World Women's Conference, Beijing 1995). Both men and women face violence; however an overwhelming majority of victims of sexual assault and domestic violence is women. Gender relations are skewed of the existence of patriarchy. In common parlance patriarchy means male domination. While it is estimated that at least 3 out of every 5 women in India face domestic violence, reporting of such cases is extremely low. One of the major factors for this is the culture of silence (as reported by The North East Network, 2004). Domestic violence is considered as a private matter and not to be interfered by others. Mental harassment, sexual and psychological violence are not taken into account by a majority of women.[2]

1. Legal Framework of Domestic Violence

From the perspective of legal framework there is confusion in Nagaland judicial system to determine which law will apply.

2 IOSR Journal of Humanities and Social Science (JHSS) ISSN: 2279-0837, ISBN: 2279-0845. 3/4 (Sep-Oct. 2012), 34-37.

Proponents of Article 371(A) of the Indian Constitution[3] claim that "customary law of the Nagas" will apply in determining a case, be it civil or criminal. However, the term "customary law of the Nagas" is a myopic and fall short of any credible clarity. This can be attributed to various reasons, first there is disparity in the customary practices of the Nagas; each tribe has sets of traditional beliefs and norms which are different from other tribes; second, there is a problem of interpretation (inconsistency) as it is based on oral tradition and without codification; third, there is a conflict of law as customary laws differ from each other; fourth, there is no procedural guidelines to determine the course of the legal decisions.

1.1. *International Law on Domestic Violence*

Articles 1 and 2 of the UN Declaration on the Elimination of Violence against Women provide the most widely used definition of violence against women.

Article One: The term "violence against women" means any act of gender-based violence that results in, or is likely to result in, physical, sexual or psychological harm or suffering to women, including threats of such acts, coercion or arbitrary deprivation of liberty, whether occurring in public or in private life.

Article Two: Violence against women shall be understood to encompass, but not be limited to the following:

i) Physical, sexual and psychological violence occurring in the family, including battering, sexual abuse of female children in the household, dowry-related violence, marital rape, female genital mutilation and other traditional practices harmful to women, non-spousal violence and violence related to exploitation;
ii) Physical, sexual and psychological violence occurring within the general community, including rape, sexual abuse, sexual harassment and intimidation at work, in

---

3 Article 371A says: (1) Notwithstanding anything in this Constitution, - (a) no Act of Parliament in respect of - (i) religious or social practices of the Nagas, (ii) Naga customary law and procedure, (iii) administration of civil and criminal justice involving decisions according to Naga customary law.

educational institutions and elsewhere, trafficking in women and forced prostitution;

iii) Physical, sexual and psychological violence perpetrated or condoned by the State, wherever it occurs.

1.2. *Indian Laws on Domestic Violence*

The Protection of Women from Domestic Violence Act 2005 defines forms of domestic violence as stated below:

Physical violence: Physical injury is the most visible form of domestic violence. The scope of physical domestic/intimate partner violence includes slapping, pushing, kicking, biting, hitting, throwing objects, strangling, beating, threatening with any form of weapon, or using a weapon. Worldwide, the percentage of women who suffer serious injuries as a result of physical domestic violence tends to range from 19% - 55%. Physical injuries as a result of domestic violence against women are more obvious than psychological ones, and can be more easily discerned by health professionals as well as courts of law in the context of legal prosecution.

Emotional abuse: Emotional has been gaining more and more recognition in recent years as an incredibly common form of domestic violence (and therefore a human rights abuse) within the private home throughout developing nations such as India. Psychological abuse can erode a woman's sense of self-worth and can be incredibly harmful to overall mental and physical wellbeing. Emotional/psychological abuse can include harassment; threats; verbal abuse such as name-calling, degradation and blaming; stalking; and isolation.

Women who experience domestic violence overwhelmingly tends to have greater overall emotional distress, as well as disturbingly high occurrences of suicidal thoughts and attempts. According to a study by the National Centre for Biotechnology Information, suicide attempts in India are correlated with physical and psychological intimate partner violence. Of the Indian women who participated in the study, 7.5% reported attempting suicide. This correlation is supported by the high rates of domestic violence in India, although the rates differ greatly by region, individual socio-economic status and other factors.

Sexual assault: Sexual assault is another common form of domestic violence in India. Sexual violence can include a range of forceful and non-forceful acts including unwanted kissing, touching, or fondling; sexual/reproductive coercion; rape; and marital rape. Abuse is most common among men who also had extramarital affairs, and among those who had STD symptoms. Abusive sexual behaviours were also found to be correlated with an elevated rate of unplanned pregnancies. In 2013, a court in Mumbai ruled that *depriving a woman of sex* is a form of cruelty.

1.3. *Customary Law/Judiciary and Domestic Violence in Naga Context*

Generally, customary law is defined as "traditional common rule or practice that has become an intrinsic part of the accepted and expected conduct in a community, profession, or trade and is treated as a legal requirement."Customary laws are integral to tribal identity and have given some basic concepts and issues around them in order to understand the dynamics of their interface with modernity and its impact on women.

Domestic violence (also domestic abuse, spousal abuse, battering, family violence and intimate partner violence) is a pattern of behaviour which involves violence or other abuse by one person against another in a domestic context, such as in marriage or cohabitation. Intimate partner violence is domestic violence against a spouse or other intimate partner. Domestic violence can take place in heterosexual or even in same-sex relationships. Domestic violence can take a number of forms including physical, emotional, verbal, economic and sexual abuse, which can range from subtle, coercive forms to marital rape and to violent physical abuse that result in disfigurement or death. Globally, a wife or female partner is more commonly the victim of domestic violence, though the victim can also be the male partner.

In the customary laws of the Nagas, a case of domestic violence is a matter of personal relationship, a family affair not to be intruded upon by the community or by any authority. It only becomes an issue of the community when there is an extreme case of death resulting from domestic violence or from divorce. Such is the case that it is not surprising that normal domestic violence cases are not reported nor brought to the any legal jurisdiction for adjudication.

Another pertinent issue is the question of jurisdiction. If at all a family feud arising of domestic violence is brought to notice, the contest is on which jurisdiction should determine the case. Indian courts only have jurisdiction to hear cases under the IPC which follow the CRPC. Hence, the contesting parties who want to settle the matter under the customary law ends up going to *Dobashi* court or Village Council court where in most cases it leads to "compromise;" where a guilty party pays compensation or choose to promise to refrain from such action in the future after reprimand.

When there is no documented Naga Customary Law jurisprudence and when there is no legal specified provision of domestic violence in Naga Customary Law, it is difficult to bring out a case of domestic violence in the Naga context. Hearsay interpretation of what would be a customary law in relation to domestic violence may fall short of delivering justice to the victim.

Moreover, there are no procedures for adjudication of cases under Naga Customary Laws. The closest of what would be like a procedure is the "notice" to come for settlement of the case. This notice may be sent out by the village council's chairman who has the jurisdiction over the case as per the customary law.

More often than not the judgement of the case is influenced by emotion, therefore logical interpretation of the case is lacking. Religious tolerance also leads to forgiveness. The harshest of punishment is to banish the perpetrator from village or retribution by compensation do not prevent future occurrence of the violence. Compromise on grounds of religiously enforce tolerance does not mitigate or solve the problem unless counselling sessions are involved.

Any attempt in this research work is to generate discussion for case study of the domestic violence in the Naga society. More in-depth study research is required through interviews and data collection as customary law is not documented.

8

Domestic Violence in Naga Society Hidden Health Burdens

Elizabeth Imti[1]

Why men are violent and what can we do about it? The need to find an answer to this question becomes increasingly urgent. The question leads us to others, equally urgent. What kind of violence are we talking about? Which men? Can we do anything about men's violence?

The fabric of our lives is interwoven with violence. The very threads of our lives seem dyed the color 'Violence'; its pervasive influence could not be more pronounced, or harder to unravel. Some parts of the coloring are clearly visible, as in, 'He beat up his wife', or 'He raped her'. Other parts are less pronounced, as in 'He's been drinking like that for years', or 'My father never talked with anyone, even my mother', or 'He refused to see a doctor for the longest time. By the time he did it was too late'. Some shades of violence are so subtle that we barely know they exist. These shades come out in the way men walk, the way they talk to their children, and the way they relate to their bodies, to women, to their souls, and to the earth itself.

When we look at the whole fabric, we see how to create new weavings free of physical and sexual assault, free of the intimations

---

1 Dr. Elizabeth Imti is Assistant Professor in the Department of Sociology, Fazl Ali College, Mokokchung.

of violence- the anger, stress, pain and frustrations that shorten lives, destroy intimacy, alienate men from their bodies, deaden feelings, responsiveness and the general ability to act creatively.

The complexities of our personal histories, male socialization, cultural backgrounds, and present relationship to violence ended the possibility of finding any simple answer to why men are violent. However, understanding male violence promises to help create a safer world. Violence is so built into our lives that we are constantly faced with an opportunity to confront it, subvert it, heal from it, and take whatever steps possible to stop it.

The mystery in our society is not that some men are angry and violent. Looking at jobs, male roles, and images of violence around us, we expect that. What is difficult to comprehend is that there is another side to millions of nice, decent law-abiding Indian men- a side carefully hidden that can erupt into physical and sexual aggression that intimidates and destroys family members and others who are close. This violence is directed at people they love, people they live with. Like the proverbial bully, they hurt people who are generally shorter, smaller, younger, and less powerful than they are.

Men are violent not only because of personality or background, but also because we have created a society in which power is defined as the ability to control others, with violence as the ultimate form of control. Our society still upholds the idea that if you can get what you want by controlling others through verbal or emotional manipulation, financial pressure, or intellectual argument, that is best thing to do. But if none of that works, it's okay to fall back on physical force.

Why men are violent is a good question. But to end the violence we need to stop explaining it and more seriously confront it. We need to focus our attention on creating a community in which violence is unacceptable. This involves acknowledging the level of violence that exists and the damage it causes. It means challenging men to change and to raise their boys to be different. Families should intentionally create safe, loving non-violent relationships and an environment that nourishes, respects, and supports each person's integrity, growth and creative abilities. We heal and change through community action, by accepting roles as parents, partners, friends, and caretakers of the earth.

Citing statistics about the cost of male violence against women only mask the reality. We need to only open the daily newspaper to read the stories. We need only to listen to women we know talk about their experiences to know the truth.

Domestic violence takes many forms and can be classified as physical, mental, emotional, sexual, economic or psychological abuse within a household. Domestic abuse is a direct offshoot of the gender imbalance in the Indian culture. Men have always been encouraged to keep their women folks under control. Spousal violence continues to scar Indian women. Violence against women has been has pervasive, unchanging and omnipresent as patriarchy itself. "Physical violence frequently operates to maintain and establish power relations when men physically batter their partners, this behavior serve as an enforcer of men's exercise of institutional and personal power."[2]

There are positive portrayals of violence in our culture. Our movies and sports heroes use violence and are rewarded for it with power, status, money and women. The costs of violence are rarely shown. It takes years and years of enforcement, name-calling, fights, threats, abuse and fear to turn men into who they are. By adolescents, they believe that they are only two choices- they can be a man or a boy, a winner or a loser, a bully or a wimp.

"The presence of accepted male behavior within intimate relationships and within the international and organizational relations of our society have come to mean that male hostility or anger, male criticism and male disapproval serve as reminders of male physical violence and power (Dworkin,1983). Because some men rape, all women must become conscious of the power and presence of men; must consider limiting their spatial, developmental and psychic mobility; and must generally restrict their interactions with others, especially men (Brownmiller, 1975; Adams, 1989). Because some men batter women, all women must become conscious and wary of male control, hostility and anger and fearful of confronting male authority. Violent men do not exist in a vacuum. Wittingly or

2 Larry L. Tifft, *Battering of Women: the Failure of Intervention and the Case for Prevention* (Westview: Boulder, 1993), p. 13.

unwittingly, their behaviour reinforces and is reinforced by patriarchal social norms and plays an integral part in the overall system of male dominance (Adams, 1989). Thereby, serving to keep women in their subordinate place (Leidig, 1981)."[3]

Domestic violence is closely linked to manipulation and control of the victim by the perpetrator and there a whole range of ways he can accomplish this without resorting to a physical assault. All of these ways, however, override the rights, desires and emotions of the victim. The victim may be intimidated by the destruction of property, display of weapons or generally aggressive actions. Threat of violence can be as frightening as the violence itself particularly when the victim knows the perpetrator may carry out the threats. Verbal abuse of victims demoralizes a victim, making her feel worthless and unloved. Verbal abuse can result in the victim coming to see herself in those terms. She may believe that she is such a bad person that she actually deserves the violence, or such a stupid person that she cannot cope alone. Verbal abuse does serves to control the victim and to compound the effects of physical violence.

The fact that some women are able to get out a relationship before the violence descends to the bottom of the spiral of repeated abuse does not mean that those women are not affected by violence. They will still suffer a broken relationship and a loss of hope; they may well have financial difficulties and feelings of deep shame and regret. Different women are affected by domestic violence in different way but all are victims.

Dobash and Dobash (1992) comments: "It is well known that violence in the home is commonplace that women are its usual victims and men its usual perpetrator. It is also known that family is filled with different forms of violence and aggression, including physical, sexual and emotional and that violence is perpetrated by young and old alike."[4]

Mariam F. Hirsch states that "Violence or at least the fear of violence is a part of every woman's life. Each woman knows someone who has been victim of the violent episode if she herself has not been

---

3 Larry L. Tifft, *Battering of Women: the Failure of Intervention and the Case for Prevention* (Westview: Boulder, 1993), p. 14-15

4 Jeff Hearn, *The Violence's of Men* (Sage: London, 1998), p. 4

involved in one time or the other. Women are assorted everyday by their portrayal in the media and on the job by their attitudes that prevail and become actualized into messages which say, 'You are not okay because you are female'."[5]

Talking about violence against women and patriarchy, Ruth Finney Hayward says "First....gender violence is a means used by men consciously and unconsciously, to limit and control women's potential power and independence....second, it is an expression of men's sense of entitlement to privilege and power. Third.... It is an expression of men's own fears of weaknesses and powerlessness, of not being "real men". Fourth, many men forced to suppress a range of emotions that are deemed to be inconsistence with manhood, channel a range of feelings into one emotion that is socially validated for men, that is anger."[6]

Women in India, like elsewhere in the world usually face violence within the household in the form of domestic violence and outside in the form of rape. According to the NFHS-2 survey in India:

- Domestic violence among the married couples is accepted and considered normal. The survey examined the justification of wife beating under various circumstances, ranging from disobedience and disrespect to in-laws to infidelity and alcohol abuse.
- Among the most persistent circumstances in which women justify violence are those related to perceptions of non-performance of domestic duties or non-compliance with expectations.
- 40% of women justify violence if a wife neglects the house or children, but only 7% justify it if the wife's natal family did not comply with the husbands demand for money or jewellery.

5 Mariam F. Hirsch, *Women and Violence* (New York: Van Nostrand Reinhold, 1981), p. xxiii

6 Finney Ruth Hayward, *Breaking the Earthenware Jar: Lessons from South-Asia to End Violence Against Women and Girls* (Kathmandu, Nepal: UNICEF, 2000).

- Better educated and urban women are less likely to justify wife beating than are other women.
- Adolescents aged 15-19 years presumably comprising those with least autonomy are most likely to justify violence than older women.[7]

Writing her views on gender inequality in India, Ratna Sarkar has said that "the most remarkable thing about the story of woman's progress towards freedom and equality is the strange uniformity of its pattern. Whether in America, Asia, Africa or Europe, the prejudice that hampers the path of progress, the obstacles that women have to encounter and surmount are almost identical. The peculiar disability attached to women all over the world is based on religion. Political disability is also biologically defined and becomes the basis for economic and social disabilities."[8]

Nagaland, the 16th state of Indian union was inaugurated on the 1st of December, 1963 with a population of hardly 3 lakhs, now it is 19.89 lakhs according to 2011 census of which 82.26% constitutes rural population. It is bounded by Assam in the North and West, by Myanmar and Arunachal Pradesh in the East and by Manipur in the South and runs more or less parallel to the left bank of the Brahmaputra river. The population of Nagaland is almost entirely tribal. There are many separate tribes and sub-tribes amongst the Nagas with their own distinctive language, customs and cultural features. More violence is noticed in this tribal society due to various factors such as technological revolution, development of townships, urbanization and modernization of tribal society in large scale. Rapid socio-economic changes have been notice ever since the statehood in 1961. The forces of globalization have entered into Naga society where mass media is playing a significant role in the family circle. The Nagas are an amalgamation of several tribes welded together with emic theories of common origin, affinity and descent and also

---

7 Domestic violence. http://w3.whosea.org/Linkfiles/Reproductive Health Profile domestic.pdf#search=%22NFHS%202%Domestic%20 violence%22.

8 Ratna Sarkar, "Gender Inequality in India: An overview", *Social Defence* 53/152 (April 2002), p. 9.

with similarity in religious ethos, rituals and practices. The interest and concern of Nagas center around family, clan and village.

1. The Status of Women in Naga Society

The colourful people of Nagaland have a rich cultural heritage and tradition. Nagaland is a home to at least 16 major and many more minor tribes. Most of these communities are ethnically similar having derived from an original common stock but their geographical isolation from each other have brought amongst them certain distinctive characteristics in language, dress and customs. Among tribes it has been observed that the family ties are an important integrating factor. Being a patriarchal society, Naga families generally consists of the husband who is the head of the family, wife and unmarried children. Naga male has all the vested powers, duties and the responsibilities. According to M. Horam, "The position of women in Naga society is far from secondary or subordinate. Majority of domestic affairs are in her hand. Laziness is a luxury among these hard-worked or to be nearer the truth over-worked women."[9]

The average age of girls at marriage in Nagaland is 22-23 years. However in some interior areas; it is common to have girls married at 15-16 years of age. Early marriage and high fertility rates have contributed to a very high decadal growth in Nagaland. Women traditionally marry within their own tribes, a practice that is still common today. Men traditionally paid dowry to the family of the bride at the time of marriage in the form of livestock's. Rooted in the tradition and governed by a general culture of care, the valuing of the girl child has continued till today.

Naga traditions that are in favour of women are equal care for the girl child, no dowry deaths, right to divorce husband anytime, specified roles in rituals and ceremonies, female feticide is unheard of, no starvation deaths, etc. The Naga traditions that are not in favour of women are that they are excluded from any decision making process, they have no inheritance of landed ancestral property and no independent income etc. Naga women however educated she may be, has no say in the tribal courts and customary laws. It is an entirely

9 M. Horam, *Naga Polity* (Delhi: B.R., 1975), p. 46.

male domain. The birth of a male child is always more welcomed and there are instances of remarriages taking place, as the woman is unable to bear a male heir even in this day and age.

Shimreichon Luithni has pointed out that, "Despite women being highly educated and occupying important positions, political parties and organizations are dominated by men. Less than a handful of women are in electoral politics. This reflects Naga women's position in decision making where they have no say. Women may have some influence at the family level but in most cases, it is the man who takes the decision. At the village level, women also have no place in the traditional village council. This applies to almost all the tribal communities of the Indian subcontinent".[10]

2. Status of Women in Angami Nagas

Among tribes it has been observed that the family tie is an important integrating factor. Naga family is without exception strictly and purely patriarchal. The Nagas consider marriage as a vitally sacred institution of society. Marriage alliances are generally settled by the parents, although with time, individuals have been given considerable freedom in choosing their partners. Marriage within the clan is strictly forbidden under their unwritten customary code. The Angamis are one of the largest group of Naga tribes. The Angamis do not have a bride price but it is their custom to offer some presents to the parents of the girl. They are monogamous people. Only sons inherit the property of their father.

The status of an Angami woman as compared to the status of a man is lower. Yet, she is seen as playing a most vital role in the family, quietly rendering great service and indirectly helping in removing poverty, fulfilling her duties and handing down a healthy tradition of hard work. The mother has no small role to play in running the family. Majority of domestic affairs are in her hands. Laziness is a luxury among these overworked women.

In Lucy Zehol's edited book we find, "Women enjoy the least privileges. The daughter is not entitled to own any of the ancesteral

10 Shimreichon Luithni, "Naga Women: A Struggle for Human Rights," *Indigenous Women: The Right to a Voice: International Work Group for Indigenous Affairs, edited by Diana Vinding* (Copenhagen: n.p. 1998), p. 124.

property (land, houses etc). This property is called "*siephruo*" which can be owned only by the male child. If the woman is an only child, the ancestral property will be given to her father's immediate relatives. This possession of ancestral property by next of kin is called "kayie". However, property bought by the parents themselves can be given to the daughter and she also can be dispose it off at her own will. This system remains rigid even today inspite of the many changes".[11]

"Divorce was quite liberal in the pre-Christian society. The existing rules are quite biased against women. A woman who cannot adjust or who wants to leave her husband will be allowed to leave for her parent's house only with her "*neikhro*" (a short white lungi). Other than that, whatever she had brought to her husband's house (ornaments, clothing., etc.) will be confiscated by her husband and the marriage becomes null and void. Whereas, a husband can leave his wife without any condition to his property. With the advent of Christianity, many changes have come about in Naga society. Unlike the traditional norm, even divorce rules has become more rigid with the Christian tradition."[12]

3. Status of Women in Chang Nagas

The Chang Nagas are one of the most important tribes of the eastern frontiers of Tuensang, Nagaland. Along with the challenges of inaccessibility, poor infrastructure, low literarcy, insurgency and poverty, Tuensang has faced problems of drug addiction, STD infections, HIV/ AIDS and marital abuse. The porous 159 km international border along the Golden Triangle has placed the young women and men at great risk. Tuensang has had one of the highest prevalence of STD, IVD use and HIV/ AIDS in the state.

A chang woman enjoys a better status than women in many other non-tribal societies. She is an equal partner to her husband in his economic pursuits. Her contribution in the domestic activities provides her with a secured place in the family. A chang woman is denied political power. She cannot act as a village chief or a village priest. This does not alter her position in the home in any way. Some women of this society are however, adversely affected by the

11 Lucy Zehol, ed., *Women in Naga Society* (New Delhi: Regency, 1988), p. 55.

12 Ibid., 57

institution of polygamy and the easier way of divorce resulting in the frequent marriage of some males. Also, another trend that is affecting the women are the instances of abuse when she is tested positive for HIV/AIDS and the husband refuses to go for testing.

Marital abuse and the causes associated with it have been different in different parts of the state. HIV/AIDS, drug abuse, economic differences and alcoholism are the causes of this problem in different Naga households. As in other patriarchal societies and in some tribal communities, which practiced patriarchy, women were socialized into being silent about their experience of violence. Traditional norms, customs and societal pressures teach them to accept, tolerate and rationalize domestic violence. This has been a significant barrier to the empowerment of women as it lowers her self esteem.

Incidents of dowry deaths, female infanticides and neglect of girl child are absent in Naga culture. However, other forms of violence like wife beating, verbal abuse, rape and molestation are on the increase and are being reported in recent years. This rising negative trend is a matter of serious concern for a tribal society where such crimes were unheard of till recent times. There are several reasons why it is impossible to obtain a completely accurate picture of how widespread the incidence of domestic violence really is in Nagaland. It is all too easy for domestic violence to remain a hidden crime, known about only by the parties involved. By definition, it will take place behind closed doors. Victims feel misplaced, shame or guilt at being a victim. Some are constantly told by their abusers that they bring the violence upon themselves, and eventually this message becomes internalized. Others are so isolated or are amongst friends and family who do not have a realistic view of domestic violence and have no one in whom they can confide. Thus, many incidents of domestic violence among Naga women remain a secret. The culture of silence leads to statistics more likely to be on the low side than on the high side.

4. Impact of Domestic Violence on Women's Health

Gender based violence is closely tied to women's sexuality, fidelity, pregnancy and child bearing. This is what makes it a reproductive health problem, as well as a physical and emotional one. Violence can lead to unwanted pregnancies, pregnancy complications, miscarriages, early labour, low birth-weight babies and maternal deaths. Many surveys have shown that assaults against women actually escalate during and after pregnancy, or during arguments over family planning. Mental and physical abuse can also affect pregnancy outcomes. Stress and trauma can induce pregnancy complications. Worse than the physical pain is the emotional anguish that a victim undergoes. This scars her for life. Emotional abuse is sometimes used as a first step in objectifying and justifying violence against another person.

A Summary Report of a Multi-Site Household Survey, 2003 found that in India 43.5 percent of women reported that they were psychologically abused by their partners, and 40.3 percent reported that they were physically abused. Fifty percent of women who were physically abused reported violence during pregnancy.[13] "Physical violence in intimate relationship is often accompanied by psychological abuse, and it is accompanied by sexual abuse in one-third to one-half of all cases."[14] "Domestic violence limits women's ability to access health care, including prenatal care and testing for HIV/ AIDS, as abusive partners often prevent women from seeking such care."[15] "A history of abuse puts women at increased risk of long-term negative health consequences including depression, suicide, chronic pain syndromes, psychosomatic disorders and sexually transmitted diseases."[16] A World Development Report titled Investing in Health has come out with the finding that women who

---

13 Domestic Violence in India: A Summary Report of a Multi-Site Household Survey, 2003, International Centre for Research on Women, Washington D.C.

14 Lori Heise, Mary Ellsberg, Megan Gottemoeller, *Ending Violence Against Women: Population Reports,* Series L No.11 (Baltimore, Maryland:, John Hopkins University School of Public Health, Population Information Program, 1999).

15 *Just Die Quietly: Domestic Violence and Women's Vulnerability to HIV in Uganda, Human Rights (*New York: Watch, Ny, 2003).

16 Etienne Krug, Linda Dalhberg; James Mercy, et al. eds. *World Report on Violence and Health* (Switzerland, Geneva: WHO, 2002).

are abused run twice the risk of miscarriage and four times the risk of having a baby that is below average weight.[17]

Gender based violence impacts women's health because it restricts their overall development directly and indirectly. The consequences of violence can lead to depression and psychological breakdown, besides all the above mentioned complications. It creates a sense of insecurity in them. It is possibly the most hurting, humiliating and the least addressed or redressed. Because it takes place within the home, it is very invisible and considered a private affair.

A. Sen feels that, "Socially, violence has been rendered invisible as people look away from it rather than confront it. The woman is silenced, as traditionally it has been believed that she dishonours the family by bringing what is private into the realm of the public. Hence, a woman is very isolated in facing violence and her subjugation is reinforced both within the family and society."[18]

Leonore E. Walker, an American psychologist who founded the Domestic Violence Institute, documented the cycle of abuse and wrote *The Battered Woman,* for which she won the Distinguished Media Award in 1979, found that battered women frequently:

- Had low self esteem.
- Accepted responsibility for the batterer's actions.
- Suffered from guilt yet denied the anger and terror they felt.
- Presented a passive face to the world.
- Had severe stress reactions with psycho physiological complains.
- Had traditional views about home and family.
- Believed that no one could solve the predicament except themselves.[19]

In our most intimate relationships we expect and are expected to love, nurture and empower one another. Yet violence and violent

---

17 *World Development Report: Investing in Health* (Oxford/New York: World Bank, 1993).

18 A. Sen, *Resources, Values and Development* (Cambridge: Mass, 1984), p. 147.

19 Leonore E. Walker, in S. L. Johann and F. Osanka, eds. *Representing Battered Women Who Kill* (Springfield, Ill.: Thomas, 1989), p. 170.

interaction patterns are generally accepted and woven into the fabric of these intimate relationships. Women who survive repeated battering episodes alternate between hoping that their situation will improve and the feeling that they can do nothing about it. As time goes by they become convinced that they are to blame for whatever problems anyone in the family is experiencing. Consequently they try harder to please. Her focus in life becomes her partner, her identity, her existence, her fate and her needs become defined in his terms. She is unable to leave him as she feels he needs her that only she can understand.

"Women need to learn that there is no cause for shame, and that if they are assaulted, they must take action-court action. As with rape and many other violent situations, women tend to blame themselves, and take on a burden of guilt which is inappropriate. They must realize that to be victimized is not to be guilty".[20] Bela Rani Sharma opines that, "Cultural differences in gender socialization affect a woman's perceptions of abuse, their ability to access services and their expectations of family support. The issue of domestic abuse is a particularly subversive one".[21] The cost of violence is borne by all, the survivor, her family, friends and society at large.

Domestic violence is more than a series of violent incidents; it's about lives saturated with fear and devaluation. Early in the marriage, after a violent incident the woman leaves to go to her natal family for help or refuge. Initially they are fairly sympathetic and take her in. She returns to her marital family a few hours or days later. As she goes back and forth, her natal family becomes less and less welcoming- they may force her to return to her marital home rapidly; and even abusive – refusing to feed her and/ or her children. Thus, the periods of respite become shorter at best and abusive at worst. Members of the family in the marital home abuse the woman with greater impunity because they see how the natal family is rejecting her. They derive validation from the natal family's abuse; and make her feel that even they think it's her fault.

---

20 Maria Roy, ed., *Battered Women: A Psychological Study of Domestic Violence* (New York: Van Nostrand Reinhold, 1977), p. 119.

21 Bela Rani Sharma, *Women- Marriage, Family, Violence and Divorce* (Jaipur: Mangal Deep, 1997), p. 106.

Eva Figes is of the view that , "when a marriage founders a wife is risking not only the loss of a lover and companion but her home and her whole way of life, and subconsciously this makes her cling to a man she might have otherwise rejected or released long ago. Modern psychologists note that women are more child like, more emotional and show a greater degree of dependence and the reason is still the same".[22]

Thus, we see that health is a holistic concept comprising both physical and mental aspects. "A woman's well being is often perceived as a negotiation of a complex set of relations between the body and the larger socio-political economic environment".[23]

Domestic violence is not just about the battering of a body. It is about the systematic destruction of the whole person. It is about the theft of hope and self confidence and about foisting on victims a skewed perception of themselves as seen from the abuser's own glazed eyes.

What causes domestic violence? What motivates those who abuse their partners? Is it their conscious choice or is it inherent in their upbringing or personality? Why does it affect some families but not others? Is it down to the individuals involved or does the responsibility lie with the society as a whole? On the surface there is no simple answer to the question, "What causes domestic violence?" Various theories have been put forward.

Marital violence differs from other forms of violence precisely because it does not appear suddenly between strangers, but always within the framework of a privileged relationship where the power equations between two people are not evenly balanced. This kind of relationship implies the use of power, physical strength, threat and intimidation. At the end of the scale, there is threat and intimidation. At the other, there is death.

The family violence perspective seeks to define the cause of marital violence as stemming from the personal characteristics of the

22 Eva Figes, *Patriarchal Attitudes: Women in Society* (London: Virago, 1978), p. 184.

23 Pauline B. Bart, Eileen Geil Moran, ed., *Violence Against Women: The Bloody Footprints* (California: Sage, 1993), p. 269.

wife or husband or in the internal and external stress that affect the family.

The patriarchal theory is closely associated with the feminist perspectives on domestic violence. Writers such as the Dobashes, claim that the phenomenon of wife abuse should be regarded not as abnormal or deviant behaviour. "Rather, it is a form of behaviour which has existed for centuries as an acceptable and indeed, desirable part of a family system within a patriarchal society."[24] Those who agree to this theory argue that our society is male dominated and that power is vested in men to dominate and to control women. They also argue that society lets men use whatever means are necessary to retain that authority should a woman dare to challenge them. Patriarchism can be seen as a collection of cultural values which govern family life.

The Status inconsistency theory holds that domestic violence is born of the frustration that occurs when the abuser perceives his status within the home as being lower than it should be. This is especially so when the abusers power has eroded whilst the victim's has increased. Often this power is financial- perhaps the abuser was always the breadwinner but now he is unemployed and he has to live off his wife's earnings. Or perhaps the abuser has a higher education than his job demands.

This theory is based on the idea that frustration, caused by such inconsistencies in status, builds up and is eventually taken out on the victim. It is more useful to look at the theory as an example of cultural values which tie in with domestic violence.

Domestic violence is caused by the cumulative effects of cultural values, the cultural legitimization of violence and the individual characteristics of abusers when they combine in particular circumstances or situations.

Most victims of domestic violence you would never notice, they are visibly strong, successful, skilled and productive individuals in the public eye. They stand by together as a portrait of the perfect family. But once indoors, in the privacy of their homes, they cower

24 R. E. Dobash and R. P. Dobash, "Wives: The Appropriate Victims of Domestic Violence," in *Victimology: An International Journal*, 2 (1978): (314), pp. 426-42.

with fear. As one person put it "I am living in hell from one day to the next. But there is nothing I can do to escape. I don't know where I would go if I did. I feel utterly powerless, and that feeling is my prison. I entered of my own free will, I locked the door, and I threw away the key." Those angry men who sit in a room and you can feel it: the simmer, the sense of some unpredictable force that might, at any moment, break loose, and do something terrible.

To quote Ravi Zacharias "There are four absolutes we all have in our minds: love, justice, evil, and forgiveness. It is easier to hide behind philosophical arguments, heavily footnoted for effect, than it is to admit our hurts, our confusions, our loves, and our passions in the marketplace of life's heartfelt transactions."

Thus, it is a matter of deep concern that violence or even its threat, inhibits women from playing an active or visible role in decision making in households, workplace or public and social spheres. Violence is understood as a structural tool to subjugate women and to keep them under male control. Today, domestic violence is no longer invisible. Both the government and the NGOs no longer harbour myths of safe and secure homes. Sustained campaigns against rapes, bride burning, sexual harassment, degrading media portrayals, domestic violence, etc., have all contributed to making violence against women a political issue.

9

The Impact of Domestic Violence on Children

Razouselie Lasetso[1]

Introduction

Domestic violence is a phenomenon that is widespread among all cultures, religions, class, and societies. It is generally defined as an act in which one person in the relationship chose violent means to intimidate the other or even hurt them. It ". . . generally occurs as a pattern of coercive power and control."[2] It is usually the strongest in the family who victimizes the weakest. Thus, the largest amount of abuse is directed against younger children. In the spousal relationship this pattern holds true that the stronger, the husband abuses the weaker, the wife. In such a context of a family where the wife has less power due to lack of education, or lack of status or lack of money, or lack of social connections the woman is said to be exposed to higher risk.[3] There are also instances where the abuse takes place the other way round in which the man is abused by the woman. But it

---

1 Dr. Razouselie Lasetso is Associate Professor, Department of New Testament, Eastern Theological College, Jorhat.

2 "What is Domestic Violence? Who is Affected by Domestic . . ." www.domesticviolence.com.au/files/ pdf/Info-Book-Final.pdf (accessed on 27/10/2014).

3 Monica McGoldrick, Mary Anne Broken Nose, Mildred Potenza, "Violence and the Family Life Cycle," *The Expanded Family Life Cycle: Individual, Family, and Social Perspectives*, third edition, edited by Betty Carter and Monica McGoldrick (Boston: Allyn and Bacon, 1999), 471.

has been established that domestic violence as a social issue largely occurs in a heterosexual relationship in which the husband victimizes the wife.[4] Therefore, for the purpose of this research focus is made on domestic violence in a heterosexual relationship in which children are adversely affected.

1. Understanding Domestic Violence

It must be noted that domestic violence, contrary to popular understanding, is not caused by frustration, stress, poverty, alcohol or drug abuse, though it is true that they may aggravate violence in the context of an existing violent family setup. It is also not an issue of anger rather it is a set of behaviour which strives to hold dominance against the other.[5] "Perpetrators of domestic violence believe they are entitled to control their family members."[6] This indicates attitude problem or misconception of role play in family setup.

1.1. *Forms of Domestic Violence*

Domestic violence in itself is very a complex phenomenon. It is not only about the abuser battering or shouting at the victim. Rather, as it has been observed:

> Domestic violence can take many different forms, some of them very subtle. Examples of domestic violence include: name-calling or putdowns, isolation from friends, family, and the community, withholding money, actual or threatened physical harm, sexual assault, stalking, and intimidation. The behaviours escalate over time. Domestic violence can be practiced in plain view of the public eye, but more often, it is kept in the confines of a home. It is often hidden by both the perpetrator and the victim to avoid any legal or personal consequences.[7]

Domestic violence is therefore widely characterized by fear, intimidation, verbal abuse, physical abuse, emotional abuse, social

---

4 *Through Their Eyes: Domestic Violence and Its Impact on Children.* Moving Women and Families Forward. www.ywcaworks.org (accessed on 28/10/2014).

5 *Through Their Eyes: Domestic Violence and Its Impact on Children.*

6 Ibid.

7 Ibid.

abuse, economic abuse, sexual abuse, controlling behaviours, spiritual abuse, separation violence, stalking, and spousal homicide.[8]

1.2. *Statistics on Domestic Violence*

In the absence of an established system of mechanism of tapping information and drawing statistics in India or in the region accompanied by a strong sense of culture-ism and religious beliefs many domestic violence occurring in the region goes unreported. Therefore, in the absence of concrete statistical evidence in the country/region it is hard to understand the subject matter as a serious social issue confronting families and societies in the country/ region. But a look at the statistics given by the American Psychiatric Association tells of the gravity of domestic violence and how it affects children's development. The statistics given below is for the purpose of our understanding the core of the issue.[9]

- One in every four women will experience domestic violence in her lifetime.
- One in 33 men have experienced and attempted or completed rape.
- An estimated 1.3 million women are victims of physical assault by an intimate partner each year.
- The majority (73%) of family violence victims are female. Females were 84% of spousal abuse victims.
- The cost of intimate partner violence exceeds $5.8 billion each year, $4.1 billion of which is for direct medical and mental health services.
- Boys who witness domestic violence are twice as likely to abuse their own partners and children when they become adults.
- 95% of batterers are men.
- A woman is battered at least once every 15 seconds in the US.

8 "What is Domestic Violence? Who is Affected by Domestic . . ."

9 "Let's Talk Facts About Domestic Violence." American Psychiatric Association. www.soc.iastate. edu/sapp/DomesticViolence.pdf (accessed on 29/10/2014).

- At least 60% of men who batter grew up in homes where they were beaten or witnessed parental battering.
- Every day, 4 women are murdered by boyfriends or husbands.
- Prison terms for killing husbands are twice as long as for killing wives.
- 93% of women who killed their mates had been battered by them.
- 67% killed them to protect themselves and their children at the moment of murder.
- 25% of all crime is wife assault.
- 70% of men who batter their partners either sexually or physically abuse their children.
- 73% of battered women seeking emergency medical services have already separated from the abuser.
- Women are most likely to be killed when attempting to leave the abuser. In fact, they are at a 75% higher risk than those who stay.
- The number-one cause of women's injuries is abuse at home. This abuse happens more often than car accidents, mugging, and rape combined.
- 60% of all battered women are beaten while they are pregnant.
- 2/3 of all marriages will experience domestic violence at least once.
- 50% of the homeless women and children in the U.S. are fleeing abuse.
- Family violence kills as many women every 5 years as the total number of Americans who died in the Vietnam War.

The above and such statistic in reality may be misleading, especially in regard to domestic violence because domestic violence is often characterised by secrecy and denial. But whatever, the sad truth is that domestic violence is common phenomenon. It is often ignored, unrecognised or suffered silently.[10] But what statistics portray

10 Hubert Anderson, D. S. Browning, I. S. Evison, M. S. V. Leeuwen (eds), *The Family Handbook* (Louisville, KY: Westminster John Knox Press, 1998), 164.

is the evil that domestic violence breeds. It breeds fear, it injures, it hurts, it makes people to flee from home, it breaks marriages, it manipulates, it kills, and it harms children's overall development. Thus, the devastating effect of domestic violence is massive.

2. Role of Religion and Culture in Domestic Violence

As noted earlier the strong belief that the perpetrators of domestic violence bear the privilege of controlling their family members fuels the problem. Such a belief is often influenced by religious and cultural practices or sanctions. Abusers often use their religion or culture as an excuse to use violence against their wives and children. But one need to note that religion cannot be made the reason for domestic violence. Observe the view below:

There is nothing to support the view that it is God's will for people to endure family violence. Use of Scripture to justify domestic violence is unacceptable. Some women may feel pressure from their faith or community to 'honour' their commitment to marriage and stay in the abusive relationship. They may think that to leave or get divorce is against their religious beliefs. 'The Scriptures can sometimes be misused to condone the use of power and to keep women and children in unsafe situations, hence care offered by the church has often been destructive rather than liberating' (Ian George, Archbishop of Adelaide, 1995).[11]

Domestic violence is a worldwide phenomenon in which some perpetrators claim that culturally women are inferior and subordinate to men and violence is allowed to keep them under control.

> In Arab and Islamic countries, domestic violence is not yet considered a major concern despite its increasing frequency and serious consequences. Survey in Egypt, Palestine, Israel and Tunisia show that at least one out of three women is beaten by her husband. The indifference to this type of violence stems from attitudes that domestic violence is a private matter and, usually, a justifiable response to misbehaviour on the part of the wife. Selective excerpts from the Koran are used to prove that men who beat their wives are following God's commandments. These religious justifications, plus the importance of preserving

11 "What is Domestic Violence? Who is Affected by Domestic . . ."

> the honour of the family, lead abusers, victims, police and health care professionals to join in a conspiracy of silence rather than disclosing these offenses. However, a fair reading of the Koran shows that wife abuse, like genital mutilation and 'honour killings' are a result of culture rather than religion (Douki et al., 2003).[12]

Similarly, Christianity that emphasizes the headship of the family upon the fathers, and women and children seen as subordinates, compounded by a strong patriarchal culture, can also be considered as one of the underlying factors contributing to domestic violence. In this sense, domestic violence in the first place is elicited by influences of religious and cultural sanctions. Therefore, in dealing with domestic violence these aspects of the problem cannot be ignored/overlooked.

3. Impact on Children

Domestic violence is not only about intra-parental conflict. It is about the disintegration of the smallest and the most significant social unit which impacts negatively all the members of the family and society. As observed, "domestic violence creates a culture of fear and intimidation that can affect every member of a family. In his quest for control, the abuser forces everyone within the range of his authority to respond to his behavior. This often includes any children who are in the home."[13] Also, "studies have shown that there is significant overlap between domestic violence and child abuse – homes where one is present are likely to have the other. The majority of studies have found that from 30 to 60 percent of families where child maltreatment or woman battering is identified, it is likely that both forms of abuse exist."[14]

Homes characterized by domestic violence are realms where children are put at high risk of physical, emotional and sexual abuse. Whether physically abused or not children in such context suffer high level of emotional and psychological problems. And it has also

12 Sibnath Deb, *Children in Agony: A Source Book* (New Delhi: Concept Publishing Company, 2006), 29.

13 *Through Their Eyes: Domestic Violence and Its Impact on Children.*

14 Ibid.

been established by researchers that the perpetrators of violence against the partner is likely to assault their children.[15] In this sense, violence against partner predates violence against children. Children in domestic-violence-ridden families suffer violence or abuse in a number of ways. First, "a child living in an environment where domestic violence occurs is an abused child" although, "not all children are affected by domestic violence in the same way."[16] Almost 90% of children in violent homes witness violence meted out against their mother. And such children witnessing violence at home are hurt psychologically and they often evidence behavioural, physical and emotional problems.[17]

Older children are often at risk of getting hurt or assaulted when they try to intervene in a violent conflict between parents. Children sometimes become victims of flying objects hurled at each other by the warring parents. Thus, they are victimized in intra-parental conflicts. Older children generally adapt themselves to strategies to cope with the violence. But younger children who are still young to understand or devise strategies are confused by the violent acts at home and they affect them adversely in their whole round developmental aspects – sometimes leading to the need for medical intervention. Some of the common reactions children from violent family setup manifest are; depression, isolation, fear, grief, eating and sleeping disorders, defencelessness, guilt, health problems, embarrassment, helplessness, poor performance in studies, drop-out, fear and shame of bringing friends home, low-self esteem, running away or staying away from home, poor decision making or judgment, violent outbursts, suicidal tendencies, alcohol or substance abuse to drown their grief and hurt, poor communicator, poor in establishing relationships, experiencing nightmares etc.[18] The list goes on. What is implied in these reactions is the extent of harm domestic violence bears on children and their future.

Children coming from homes characterized by domestic violence are thus impacted negative in many and varied ways. This can

15 "What is Domestic Violence? Who is Affected by Domestic . . ."

16 Ibid.

17 Ibid.

18 Ibid.

be roughly classified in the following ways under each developmental criterion:

a. ***Behavioural, Social and Emotional Affects:*** They are more likely to be aggressive and display antisocial behaviours than children coming from normal homes. They are characterized by depression and anxiety, displaying high levels of anger, hostility, disobedience and unacceptable behaviours. They may exhibit mood swings, temperamental problems, regressed or fearful behaviour. They are usually withdrawn with low self-esteem, and are poor in building relationships,[19] and have less social competence and poor choice of friends. They are likely to get involved in anti-social activities, alcohol or drug experimentation, premature sexual activity[20] and even run away from home.
b. ***Cognitive and Attitudinal Affects:*** They are usually affected in their motor, verbal and cognitive development and turn to be poor in studies and as such perform or score badly in schools and social life. They reflect intellectual, learning and concentration problems. They lack conflict resolution skills, and are slow in problem solving skills. They usually hold onto pro-violent attitudes and believe in strong gender roles.[21]
c. ***Physical/Health Affects:*** Abusive violence towards children in a domestic-violent family setup bears a high risk of harming the child physically. They experience sleep disorders and nightmares. They exhibit developmental delays. They face mental illnesses such as headaches, stomach pains, speech impediment etc. The acts of

19 "Domestic Violence and the Child Welfare System," *Bulletin for Professionals*, Oct. 2009, www.childwelfare.gov.

20 Freddy Cardoza, "Crisis on the Doorstep," *A Theology for Family Ministries*, edited by Michael & Michelle Anthony (Nashville, TN: B. & H. Academic, 2011), 47.

21 Brown & Bzostek, 2003; Edelson, 2006. Cited in "Domestic Violence and the Child Welfare System," Bulletin for Professionals, Oct. 2009, www.childwelfare.gov.

violence may include ". . . kicking, biting, punching, hitting or trying to hit a child with an object, beating up a child, burning or scolding, and threatening or using a gun or a knife."[22]

d. ***Spiritual Affects:*** Through parents' relationship with their children parents participate in the children's spiritual formation. Therefore, the experience of unconditional love and grace on the part of the parents towards children is most encouraged in the formation of the child's spirituality. Most children are said to perceive that God is like their parents and other adults who play a significant role in their life. Those who receive good gifts from parents and family see God a one who gives good gifts as well. But acting contrary to their expectation of a good and loving God often impairs children's understanding of God.[23] Domestic violence can have severe spiritual consequences on the child as the child may tend to distrust God. But it is also true that in some cases children who have personally accepted Jesus Christ draw closer to him in seeking refuge from him in a violent family setup.

e. ***Long Term Affects:*** The effect of domestic violence is usually not short term, specific or time bound. Rather, "family violence has a long-lasting negative impact on the children. Its consequences can be devastating. As a result of being abused or neglected, children may also exhibit behaviours such as aggression, provocative behaviour, or withdrawal that could lead to more abuse."[24] It has been argued that not all children from domestic violent homes become violent themselves in the future. However, statistic shows that around 30% of the abuse children turn out to become violent when they grow up. The long term effect here is that boys from such families are more likely

---

22 Sibnath Deb, *Children in Agony: A Source Book*, 21.

23 Scottie May, Beth Posterski, Catherine Stonehouse, and Linda Cannell, *Children Matter: Celebrating Their Place in the Church, Family and Community* (Grand Rapids, MI: Wm B. Eerdmans Publishing Company, 2005), 152-153.

24 Sibnath Deb, *Children in Agony: A Source Book*, 22.

> to involve in domestic violence as adults. And contrary to this girls usually turn out to become victims of domestic violence. Thus, "exposure to domestic violence is . . . also one of the several adverse childhood experiences (ACEs) that have shown to contribute to premature death, as well as risk factors for many of the most common causes of death in the United States."[25]

Apart from all the damages children receive in terms of emotion, physical, social, spiritual and behavioural, they also tend to come to believe that it is okay to be violent to get what you want and such belief can lead the child to continue a cycle of violence when they build their own family.[26]

The role of the family is to provide a conducive environment where the children can be nurtured with care and support to grow and develop under normal circumstances. Violence and abuse are contrary to this expectation. They rather hinder the friendly environment and affect the child adversely. Therefore, domestic violence and abuse need to be addressed with all sincerity.

4. Intervention Strategies

Addressing the issue of domestic violence and its related issues is complex and varied. No single intervention strategy can address the complexities of domestic violence each violence- ridden family exhibits. As Deb observes,

> Although family violence and child maltreatment have been recognized as social and public health problems in both the developed and developing countries, very few measures/policies have been taken to stop all forms of family violence and cruelty towards children in the developing countries. In fact, it is very difficult to offer a single solution to curb family violence and cruelty towards children. Moreover, the cases of family violence and child maltreatment/physical abuse are not reported in the

25 "Domestic Violence and the Child Welfare System." *Bulletin for Professionals*, Oct. 2009, www.childwelfare.gov.

26 "What is Domestic Violence? Who is Affected by Domestic . . ."

developing countries. Even if reported very few actions have been taken.[27]

In India, domestic violence was recognised as a specific criminal offence in 1983 which led to the introduction of section 498-A into the Indian Penal Code. Besides this India also adopted the Convention on the Elimination of All Forms of Discrimination against Women and the Universal Declaration of Human Rights which ensure protection of women. Article 15 (3) of the Indian Constitution also has a provision that empowers the legislature to make special provision for women and children. In line with this, the Protection of Women from Domestic Violence Acts was passed in 2005. The provisions covered under this act are protection from (i) physical abuse (ii) sexual abuse (iii) verbal and emotional abuse and (iv) economic abuse. The beneficiaries of this Act are women, children and Respondent.[28] Besides this, India also subscribes to the Convention on the Rights of Child as one of the signatories. This Convention enshrines that "the parents and guardians bear the primary duty and responsibility for the upbringing of children, with the necessary support of the State (arts. 5 and 18). Article 19 requires States to take all appropriate measures to protect children from all forms of violence, abuse, neglect and maltreatment, including sexual abuse while in the care of parents or legal guardians."[29]

But in spite of such provisions protecting women and children from abuse and violence people's response is not encouraging due to strong cultural factors such as patriarchy, shame and family honour. Therefore, as Deb observes, "In order to prevent family violence educational approaches for enlightenment is needed that help professionals and communities to develop more effective skills to work with families and communities."[30] Counselling the perpetrator,

---

27 Sibnath Deb, *Children in Agony: A Source Book*, 23.

28 "Domestic Violence in India: The Protection of Women from Domestic Violence Act 2005," http://www.helplinelaw.com/family-law/DVLI/domestic-violence-in-india.html (accessed on 3/11/2014).

29 "Violence against children, within the family and in schools," www.ohcr.org/EN/HRBodies/CRC/ Documents/.../school.pdf (accessed on 3/11/2014).

30 Sibnath Deb, *Children in Agony: A Source Book*, 24.

the victim and the child alone is not the answer to domestic violence and abuse. The underlying factors behind the violence such as cultural influence and religious factors must also be addressed to correct domestic violence.

It must also be noted that, "the family is the natural and fundamental group unit of society and is entitled to protection by society and the state."[31] Therefore, legality and its provisions put into place by the state for the protection of families must be invoked where applicable. In this, education and awareness campaigns must be put into place along with education on the ill effects of domestic violence upon the abused, particularly, women and developing children.

5. Theological Implications

The biblical account begins with the story of God creating Adam and Eve and putting them in the garden as companions. The creation was complete and everything and every relationship were in order until Adam and Eve disobeyed. Their rebellion had serious consequences in the relationship with God and with each other – discord was introduced. Genesis 3:16 explains the relationship that will be between them henceforth – one of dependence and dominance. This however was not a perpetual state of strife into eternity. The coming of Jesus Christ reconciles the brokenness into a newness of family life.

It is true that there are cases where women abuse men in some relationship but in majority of the abuses and domestic violence the perpetrators are men – constituting more than 90% of such cases. Such is the devastating power of sin that has engulfed family relationship. Domestic violence has characterized many human families since then. ". . . the crime of domestic violence are intrinsically and morally evil in all of their manifestations, affecting individuals and cultures in deleterious ways."[32]

---

31 Freddy Cardoza, "Crisis on the Doorstep," *A Theology for Family Ministries*, edited by Michael & Michelle Anthony (Nashville, TN: B. & H. Academic, 2011), 45.

32 Lorrie C. Reed, "Theological Reflection on Domestic Violence," http://reflectiverenewal.blogspot. in/2013/10/theological-reflection-on-domestic.html (accessed on 7/11/2014)

The Law (Torah) explicitly states the positive function of parents towards their children in passing on the faith to them as responsible parents (Deut. 11:18-21). So also Jesus talked of parents who know and do what is good for their children (Mt 7:9-11). Domestic violence involving children is against the will of God. The Psalmist exclaims that "children are a heritage from the Lord" (Psa 127:3). Children are put under the care of the parents as primary caregivers. Therefore, violence and abuse is against the divine intent of God. Paul writes to the Ephesian parents, "Fathers do not provoke your children to anger, but bring them up in the discipline and instruction of the Lord" (Eph 6:4; cf Col 3:21). Similarly, children are to obey their parents. Wives are exhorted to be subjected to their husbands as to the Lord (Eph 6:22). So also husbands are exhorted to love their wives just as Christ loved the church and gave his life for her (Eph 6:25). Husband and wife are reminded that they are no longer two but one in the flesh (Eph 6:31). Husbands are particularly reminded that they are to love their wives as they love themselves (Eph 6:33). God hates broken families which is the ultimate outcome of domestic violence in many cases (cf. Mal 2:16). The picture of God-ordained family is one where submission, love and obedience characterize the Christian family.

Conclusion

Domestic violence is chiefly a matter of choice and is a serious social concern. It seriously effects the growth and development of the child in all aspects of the child's growth: physical/motor, emotional/psychological, cognitive/intellectual, spiritual, and social skills. This clearly is not the will of God for the human family. Therefore, the issue needs to be dealt carefully and meaningfully. The effect has a long term consequence to all parties (men, women, and children), including the church, society and nation. Therefore, domestic violence as a social concern must be taken seriously. It must be dealt carefully as the soundness of the family, church, society or the nation rest largely upon the health of the family. This is truer in the context of the church in which the family is to reflect the love of God. Education of the mass, counselling of the effected and correction of religious and cultural forces or harmful traditions which fuel the violence need to be addressed in all sincerity.

10

Theological Response to Domestic Violence

Eyingbeni Hümtsoe-Nienu[1]

Introduction: Mapping the Essay

How do we respond theologically to the victims/survivors of domestic violence (DV)[2] so that they are enabled to overcome the trauma without being judged according to bias established socio-cultural norms and expectations? How do we theologically respond to the perpetrators[3] of DV in a manner that frees the victims from similar occurrences in the future and subsequently restore offenders to responsibility driven lives? Can a renewed theological construct serve as a meaningful basis for responding to DV? How can faith-based approach to peace impact positively the victims and the perpetrators of DV? These are the questions that this essay attempts to address. It primarily seeks to understand domestic violence from the point of

---

1 Dr. Eyingbeni Hümtsoe-Nienu is Senior Lecturer in Department of Christian Theology, Clark Theological College, Aolijen.

2 The other common term is "intimate partner violence". However, the preferred term in this essay is the commonly used word 'domestic violence' which is more comprehensive from a context relevant viewpoint whereby members of the household not only include 'intimate partners' like spouses or lovers but is normally comprised by a larger web of relationships including domestic help, elderly parents, and also children – both young and adults, and also relatives – both close and distant.

3 The cognate terms like "offenders" and "responsible persons" are used interchangeably in the essay.

power imbalance which leads to fractures in human relationship and to counter the cause and the effect with faith resources particularly from the framework of God's reconciling love in Jesus Christ. The method is interdisciplinary in general in that it incorporates perspectives from social sciences, peace studies and most dominantly Christian theology. The essay is premised on social constructionism[4] which is compatible with a theological "constructionism" that believes that people and situation can change for better – the experiences of the victims and actions of the perpetrators can be changed – through the reconciling love of God that enables all to embrace a restorative future.

1. Domestic Violence: Personal Witness – Starting Point of Engagement

While growing up, I accustomed frequent cases of DV. Some homes had alcoholic parents, particularly fathers, who would come home at weird hours at night and alarm the entire family. It starts with the father shouting at the mother and then onto the children. By morning members of the family either had swollen or black eyes. They've either being crying out of fear and despair or have been beaten up. Those families who had no problem of alcoholic parents had children with the issue. Normally, the alcoholic is a son who would create mayhem by breaking everything in sight – from kitchen utensils to electronic gadgets. There are times when the abusive subject is not an alcoholic but simply a person with foul temper and thinks his anger/rage/fury will some how be satisfied if he engaged in loud and aggressive behavior on the rest of the family members. I saw how a father brutally beat up his biological daughter while at the same time tying her hands and legs and leaving her above a traditional fire place (*pfüki*). I was a child and that sight still terrifies me! Some people simply make their family members easy prey as a

4 Constructionism concerns the method of understanding ontology not from a essentialist view which is rule-based but rather from the view "of ever-changing world". Inger Skjelsbæk, "Is Femininity Inherently Peaceful? The Construction of Femininity in War," *Gender, Peace and Conflict*, edited by Inger Skjelbæk and Dan Smith (London/California/New Delhi: SAGE Publications, 2001), 48, 50-52

cover-up for their perverted lifestyle. One such case is of a husband in extra-marital relationship who desperately attempted to torture the wife in the hope that the wife would leave him on her own.

The situation of DV gets more complicated in cases where those in the abusive relationship are financially dependent on the abuser; they are generally women, children, elderly and domestic helps, who are usually not in a position to confront or to walk away; so they continue to tolerate the abuse – in silence, mostly.

2. Domestic Violence: Socio-Cultural and Ecclesial Paradox

In the cultural context of the Nagas in particular and tribals of Northeast in general, there seems to be little concern against DV. The epidemic is not adequately acknowledged - neither by the community nor the Church. Despite the severity of the issue, the society appears to treat it as a personal, family, and domestic concern not to be intervened by those outside the perimeter of the home and the relationship. According to Summers and Randalls, the Northeast India region falls under the "exotic places"[5] "where domestic violence is not viewed as a crime but rather is culturally accepted as a part of everyday life."[6] Tragically, the cycle of DV is repeated when the community does nothing to address the concern or hold the perpetrator accountable for the action. In such an indifferent surrounding, the victim not only suffers physical and emotional pain, but also has to bear the brunt of community's unpleasant attention caused by the bruises (internal and external), whilst the culprit attracts no such stare – life is as normal as usual.

The victim-centered approach to domestic violence is evident in the way society questions the behavior of the victim that "invited" such act of violence upon them. When a wife is beaten up by the husband, society is wont to capitalizing on all the "negative" characteristics of the wife. When a teenage daughter is stripped and tied to a gatepost by the father for indulging in alcohol, the society ruthlessly defends the shameless act of the father with a comment like, "As a father

5 "Exotic" is distinguished from the "modern industrialized societies with progressive laws". Randal W. Summers and Allan M. Hoffman, Eds., *Domestic Violence: A Global View* (Westport, CT: Greenwood Press, 2002), xii.

6 Ibid.

he has the right to discipline her 'immoral' daughter."[7] Even in the case of child abuse, society fails to realize that they are siding with the perpetrator when they ask a question like, "What did you do to provoke your father that he beat you up so roughly?" Such responses and attitudes only perpetuate DV because the offenders' actions are implicitly rendered necessary and the victims are explicitly deemed as deserving the "punishment". Thus, socio-culturally there seems to be certain group of people who have been granted "the right to violence" over another group of people.

Tradition is the foundation of customary law, extant till date, but traditionally there seems to have been no fitting cultural mechanism to address DV although it was recognized as an unpleasant exercise of power on the part of the perpetrator. A folk story will substantiate this claim.

> *Long time ago, in one Lotha village, there lived two best friends. They would go to field together, come together and hunt together. One of the friends' wives was very pretty and the other friend was jealous of him and wanted to destroy their relationship. One day as they were making their way back from the field, one friend suggested beating up their wives to the other friend. Since they did all things together, the other friend agreed to the suggestion. Thus they made a pact to beat up their wives.*
>
> *On reaching the village the other friend heard the sound of trashing and the cry of the neighbor's wife. He presumed that his friend was being loyal to the pact. Thence he literally began to batter his wife. This act of cruelty made the wife very sad and prompted her to leave her husband. Before leaving she made a jar of rice beer and asked him to drink it on his own since she will be gone to her parents' home.*
>
> *One day, on hearing the neighbors in conflict, he quietly walked towards their house. To his surprise he saw that his friend was not actually assaulting the wife but only hitting the winnow ('moro') placed on top of a bale of cotton and that the wife was simply conspiring by mimicking a crying sound. He realized that he had*

7 Based on a true incident.

been deceived and deeply regretted his action but it was too late because the wife had already left.

He drowned himself in the rice beer which the wife had made for him. He would think of her and yearn for her. He did not survive the heartache. He died of a broken heart![8]

The story affirms that DV was viewed negatively on a personal and familial level in the ancient tribal world but the failure to make it a community concern and the inability to recognize violence within the family as "paranormal" – whether it is the case of parents spanking children, sibling getting into physical fights, mistreatment of domestic helpers and elderly, or partner and spousal battering – are disturbing. Customary laws of the Naga often address violence issues selectively. For instance, leaders of civil organizations, who are the unwritten custodians of customary/traditional laws, take cases like sexual assault, especially rape, into consideration but usually trivialize wife-battering or ignore child spanking altogether. Behavior such as those mentioned are neither openly challenged nor considered harmful and unacceptable. The family and relatives may organize a mediation program but usually it is for serving ultimatums, rebuking one or the other or both parties, making final decisions on behalf of either party or serving penalty to the perceived offender – e.g., "*If you wish to stay married, you have to stop hitting your wife or else just divorce.*" "*Both of you bring shame to the name of the family and clan.*" "*Should you misbehave again the children will be taken away from you!*" "*For the act done you have to pay a pig!*"[9]

The lack of systematic approach to DV in tribal communities extends to the tribal churches. Although tribal churches do not openly condone DV and yet by their obvious inaction they become silent collaborators with the offenders in perpetuating DV. Moreover, the glorification of silence, coupled with societal apathy, inhabits victims from speaking out and sharing with pastors. Except for select churches, there is hardly any (family) counselor in the church to whom victims

8 Oral narration by Tsenimo Humtsoe, 70 years, on November 7, 2014, Wokha Town, Nagaland, India.

9 These phrases are based on personal encounters and news items from local dailies.

can openly talk concerning their supposed "personal" business. This does not excuse the Church from engaging with the issue. Since customary laws offer no ready way out to address the concerns of DV, the idea of restoring the cracking (family) relationship on the basis of faith becomes most essential, especially when the majority of members in the society, and the victims and perpetrators are likely professing Christians.

3. Problem of Domestic Violence: Problem of Power Imbalance

The problem of DV is centered on the exercise of power and how that plays out in intimate relationships, particularly within the household members. From this perspective, violence is meted out on those who are normally power-less. Referring to violence against women, Barrie Levy, clinical social worker and faculty of UCLA, explains that "socio-cultural theories explain violence against women as stemming from social structures or cultural conditions. Advocates of these theories say that men abuse women 'because they can'."[10] She also contends that "Societies that reinforce the use of violence as a legitimate means to achieve desired ends support violence [against women]."[11] This statement is reflected clearly when offenders use violence on victims to keep them "in their place" and the society justifies that position by keeping silent. Power then gets consolidated in the offender giving way to more undue exercise of it on the 'others'.

The imbalance of power manifests itself in the way those with power, derived from any quarters of life, are wont to harming those at the other end of the power scale. Those on the powerful side are those favored by the structures of the society, namely the men, the rich, the adults, the able-bodies and the adults. Juxtaposed against this group are those disadvantaged by the structures of societies namely the women, the poor, the children, the disabled and the elderly. People of both sides normally become part of the domestic realm in which power in systemically invested in the former group. Domestic abuse, in the case of the tribals in general and Nagas in particular, is to be perceived as extrapolations of power-imbalance already evidenced in traditional tribal communities and not necessarily an entirely

10 Barrie Levy, *Women and Violence* (Berkeley, CA: Seal Press, 2008), 20.

11 Ibid.

new experience as a result of modernity. In such a case, societal (re) arrangement that produces equality and puts an end to the principle of "the right to dominate" – other face of "the right to violence" - is of primary concern.

The fact that Christianity is the religion of most of the tribal communities in the Northeast India region has not positively transformed the general quality of human relations. The ancient distinctions founded on gender, class, age, tribe, etc., continue to affect the way we relate to one another. Reflecting on the biblical story of Cain and Abel, Miroslav Volf posits that "From the outset, all human relations are fraught with the tension between equality and difference."[12] Differences seem to take precedence over equality in our tribal society even today. Between spouses there still exists the idea of man-woman differentiation; between house-owners (*maliks*) and helps the status distinction is maintained; between adults and children the sense of unrestrained authority is perpetuated by the former; between friends – platonic or romantic – undue advantages are exploited by one over the other. Such differences created by human structures are problematic in themselves as they create artificial boundaries between people. The intensity of the issue gets apparent when these artificial constructs serve as risk factors by constituting conditions of fear, oppression, assault, and the like. When such a thing occurs, the environment within the home and among close relations is nothing short of a war-like zone. Intervening in such conditions require societal will propelled not be rigid regulations and customary inclinations but by a strong sense of the need to balance power and its equal and responsible execution amongst household members.

Heather Nancarrow clearly indicates that the weakness of informal justice or community mediation is "related primarily to the imbalance of power between the victim and perpetrator of abuse and the *mediator's inability to effectively balance this power.*"[13] From the

12 Miroslav Volf, "Original Crime, Primal Care," *God and the Victim: Theological Reflections on Evil, Victimization, Justice and Forgiveness*, edited by Lisa Barnes Lampman (Grand Rapids, MI/ Cambridge, UK: Wm. B. Eerdmans/Neighbors Who Care, 1999), 25.

13 Heather Nancarrow, "Restorative Justice for Domestic and Family Violence: Hopes and Fears of Indigenous and Non-Indigenous Australian Women,"

tribal Christian standpoint domestic violence can be most effectively addressed when the community and the Church gets involved by sending out the message that DV is wrong and that such should not occur in the future. But this is possible when power is impartially administered that even victims/survivors benefit. This represents hope for those who have suffered as a consequence of the power imbalance. For the perpetrators it serves as a restrictive mechanism against repeating the offence. For both, it is a protective apparatus against reverse outcome of becoming a potential victim or offender.

4. Theological Framework: De-centralizing Power with the Tool of Reconciling Love

Theology should not support domestic violence – or any violence instigated by wrath, hatred, revenge and chauvinism. The theological task in responding to DV is de-centralizing power in the hands of the traditional lords seen today in the guise of abusive husbands, male-friends, house-owners/bosses, and adults. This involves putting the attribute of the omnipotence of God in perspective. The fact that the powerful God is nothing like any of His creation does not mean that God treats creation in a domineering manner. Far from it, His powerfulness is complemented by His love that even when He wields His judgment He does so with a restorative purpose (Jeremiah 29: 11). The power of God, then, is not a tool for abuse but a divine ontological attribute which God graciously extends to creation- particularly towards humanity- empowering them to a life of love expressed in honorable conduct towards self and others (nature included). In other words, God's omnipotence is in the least linked to absolute power than it is to absolute love. Jeremiah's witness to this love is enshrined in God's declaration, "I have loved you with an everlasting love" (Jeremiah 31:3b)[14]. The promise of covenantal restoration with Israel (v. 4-5) is prompted by the eternal love of God. Since God is eternal all that essentially characterizes God – namely, love – must naturally follow His existence. The apostle John confirms this when he declares, "God is love" (1 John 4:8b). This

---

Restorative Justice and Violence as Women, edited by James Ptacek (No Details), 128.

14 All Bible texts are from New Revised Standard Version.

essence of divinity flows out to humanity without distortion through Jesus Christ – like pure water from a spring (John 15:9 - "As the father has loved me, so I have loved you). God as the origin and fountain of love means that when God, out of love sent Jesus, He was inviting the world to a life with Himself (John 3:16). Those who accept the invitation reflect His essence of love and are marked by vertical and horizontal levels of reconciliation (2 Corinthians 5:19; John 13:34). Love then is the measure of all things (1 Corinthian 13), and among human beings love that reconciles and nourishes relationship between them is vital to perfecting the love of God (1 John 4:12b).

Power that operates exclusively in the hands of the privileged group runs contrary to the reconciling effect of God's love because relationships that are built on divine principles operate on the premise of love and not power. The saying, "Absolute power destroys absolutely" is nowhere more relevant than in the context of human relationship. DV occurs when power is concentrated and exercised absolutely by one over the other. Thus, de-centralizing power with the reconciling love of God is significant for cementing human relationship. In the context of DV it is expressed in the ability to resist negative influence of power that results in brokenness of relationship between household members. Where brokenness has already occurred, it is a tool to cement the cracks.

Hence, it is clear that the objective of the theological framework is ultimately geared towards reconciliation. Here, I take Sinclair Ferguson's interpretation of reconciliation that is built of the root word *katallage* which characterizes the idea of "one set of circumstances giving way to, and being exchanged for another."[15] Reconciliation is possible because God is love and he has taught us how to love (1 John 4:19); and love naturally has the competence to inspire reconciliation.

15 Sinclair B. Ferguson, "Preaching the Atonement," *The Glory of the Atonement: Biblical, Historical and Practical Perspectives,* edited by Charles E. Hill and Frank A. James III (Downers Grove, IL: InterVarsity Press, 2004), 432-433.

5. The Question of Principles: How does God Execute Justice to both Victims and Offenders?

Does God work exclusively in favor of the victims as the liberation theologians' slogan "God's preferential option for the poor" suggests? How does God deal with the DV offenders? How does God's reconciling love of God in Jesus put our perspective of God in place and at the same achieve a victim-offender centered response that favors both? The section below addresses the queries by understanding the dynamics of divine principles centered on the reconciling love of God.

5.1. *God's Reconciling Love Excludes Victimization*

The all-powerful God, historically speaking, has seen interpretations that project Him as violent. The classical ideas of atonement that speaks of a God whose wrath is satisfied by the vengeful death of His Son engenders a theology of, in the words of postmodern thinkers, "Murderous exchange," because "to suggest that Jesus died to pay the penalty for our sins is to suggest that God only forgives after first seeking retaliation for sin."[16] Similarly, such interpretations also have the potential to justify or even glorify suffering as marks of Christian discipleship. However, atonement when appropriately structured is far from the ideas of *satisfaction* or *penal substitution* or even *ransom*.[17] It is to be basically focused on God's essential nature expressed in love and touching His creation with it. The problem with all three classical ideas of atonement lies in their failure to comprehend the love of God which finds expression not in "exchanges" and "victimizing" but in supreme demonstrations of divine compassion.

Peace scholars have attempted to selectively condemned violence. According to Thomas Merton, violence can be condemned when it "implicitly favors the claims of the powerful and self-seeking establishment against the common good of [hu]mankind or against

16 Kevin J. Vanhoozer, "The Atonement in Postmodernity," *The Glory of the Atonement*, 372.

17 Cf., Gustav Aulen, *Christus Victor: An Historical Study of the three main types of the Idea of the Atonement* (London: SPCK, 2010 [1931]).

the rights of the oppressed"[18] On the one hand, his posture appears like a license for the marginalized to be explicitly violent without realizing that a victim is a potential offender and vice versa. On the other hand, his idea of Christian non-violence sounds painfully incriminating to victims of DV when he writes, "the key to non-violence is the willingness of the non-violent resister to suffer a certain amount of accidental evil in order to bring about a change of mind in the oppressor and awaken him to personal openness and to dialogue."[19] Violence as referring to anything that causes harm or injury is never justifiable. That is far from how God works in His scheme of reconciling work.

The biblical narratives of *Cain and Abel* (Genesis 4) and *Hagar and Sarai* (Genesis 16-18) typify a household conflict. The former portrays sibling rivalry leading to fratricide and the latter represents the multi-dimensional factors (class, gender, and ethnicity) involved in engendering DV. But both stories reveal that however and wherever power tilts the tendency to be violent seems natural – whether to exercise arbitrary power granted by the social systems or simply to exact revenge. However, it is consoling to observe God's graciousness to the power-less. In the case of Cain, his frailty is exposed when God pronounces His judgment. God could've annihilated him and satisfied the hunger of avengers but he did not act against his nature. God pronounces a protective blessing on Cain, the former offender (Genesis 4:15). Contesting René Gerard's reading of the story of Cain and Abel (Gen), who takes the perspective of the victim (Abel) and condemns the perpetrator (Cain), Miroslav Volf asserts that the significance of the story lies in its attempt to "Counter the tendency of the victim to turn into a perpetrator."[20] Similarly Hagar and Sarai, both victims and offenders simultaneously, are dignified as God frees them from their socially vulnerable conditions. The implication is

18 Thomas Merton, *Faith and Violence: Christian Teaching and Christian Practice* (Notre Dame, Indiana: University of Notre Dame, 1976 [1968]), 5.

19 Ibid., 27-8.

20 Miroslav Volf, "Original Crime, Primal Care," *God and the Victim: Theological Reflections on Evil, Victimization, Justice and Forgiveness*, edited by Lisa Barnes Lampman (Grand Rapids, MI/ Cambridge, UK: Wm. B. Eerdmans/Neighbors Who Care, 1999), 23.

that power derived from birthing a son is equally distributed between them and moreover, their sons (Ishmael and Isaac) also receive proportionate share of earthly power (Genesis 16:10-12; 17:15-20). Power equity emancipates the two women from perpetuating mutual hostility as much as it frees Cain from fear of becoming victims of circumstances. Such is the nature of God's justice. Does this mean that the offenders granted absolute impunity for their action? No!

5.2. *God's Reconciling Love includes Just-Retribution*

The tribal society as practically governed by customary unwritten laws rely on punitive actions to deal with civil and criminal cases - exacted mostly in kind and seldom in nominal cash.[21] In ethics of justice it is akin to retributive justice[22] which is not the best of responses, particularly in cases of DV. Because although God does not exonerate offenders out rightly, God also does not show himself to be balancing the books by distributive punishment in accordance with the crime committed; much like in the governmental criminal justice system.[23] So, with God it is not about reprisal but then again no one escapes his reproach. In this sense, retributive justice is irrelevant to God but just-retribution is a confirmation of His omniscient and omnipotent attributes. God's just-retribution is made explicit in ascribing blame to the guilty and ensuring that offenders accept the consequences of their offense with remorse, trusting that God is a fountain of love and will channel that love in godly fashion. The questions posed to Cain, "Where is your brother Abel?" (v. 9) and divine pronouncement of penalty on Cain, "And now you are cursed from the ground…" (v. 11) holds Cain guilty of homicide and the "price" he had to pay for the crime. God in no way demands intolerable suffering or harm on Cain as a result of even a serious crime like murder for that would

21 For a detailed list of fines in relation to offences refer Talitemjen Jamir and A. Lanunungsang, *Naga Society and Culture: A Case Study of the Ao Naga Society and Culture* (Lumami: Nagaland University, Tribal Research Centre, 2005), 69-60.

22 For characteristics of retributive justice see Howard Zehr, "Restoring Justice," *God and the Victim: Theological Reflections,* 134-5.

23 Howard Zehr, *The Little Books of Restorative Justice* (Intercourse, PA: Good Books, 2002), 59-60.

contradict the dynamic gift of God's reconciling love which is not obsessed with the past fault but rather concerned with a right future that mirrors that gift.

The Christian stance can go on to demand the admission of wrong by the offender but must not ignore to plea to God for the realization that the perpetrators not only objectifies human's hopelessness in exercising free will but, much more than that, manifests human's potential to be subjected to the evil powers. However, offenders would be wrong to rest secure in the thought that God would tolerate offenses owing to humanity's evil-prone nature. Far from it, since He expressed His perfect love in Christ He makes no excuses (Cf., John 15:22) but justly reprimands offenders to hold them responsible and at the same time initiate healing on the victims. What Zehr says in this connection is meaningful – "Restitution by offenders is often important to victims...when an offender makes an effort to make right the harm, even if only partially, it is a way of saying 'I am taking responsibility, and you are not to blame'."[24] Here the needs of the victim and the need of the offenders "to understand the consequences of their actions or to empathize with victims," are equally addressed.[25]

5.3. *God's Reconciling Love affects Restoration*

Although the story of *Cain and Abel* does not allow us to include Abel in the restorative process, for Cain, the offender, it was an immense act of restoration which God bestows on him. The idea of restoration is especially meaningful in a tribal context wherein "ex-communication" as an expulsion from the community is considered the penultimate penalty pronounced on those who have violated customary civil code in the highest degree. Some are expelled for

24 Howard Zehr, *The Little Books of Restorative Justice* (Intercourse, PA: Good Books, 2002), 15. To emphasize this aspect, RESTORE (Responsibilty and Equity of Sexual Transgressions Offering a Restorative Experience), a group from Arizona, uses the term *Responsible Person* "to label the individual who perpetrated unlawful, unwanted sexual activity instead of words such as 'perpetrator' or 'offender'. Mary P. Koss, "Restorative Justice for Acquaintance Rape and Misdemeanor Sex Crimes," *Restorative Justice and Violence Against Women*, edited by James Ptacek, 219.

25 Zehr, *Restorative Justice*, 16.

a set period of time, in some cases it can last a lifetime, albeit with relaxation, and in some instances it is rigidly enforced for life. But there are no cases of "eye for an eye; tooth for a tooth". Though the objective of tribal customary laws is generally punitive there are several tribal legends of peace-building that clearly commends restorative initiatives. The process of restoration is usually low-key. There is no celebrative music and dance or feasts as in conciliatory occasion between two belligerent villages. But the subtle joys are unmistakable in the way people open their doors and extend welcoming gestures like a handshake. And because restoration focuses on putting right by repairing the harms done and gaining closure to both victim and offender[26] they are both enable to rise above the circumstances and experience newness in their relationship.

Howard Zehr, an authority in restorative justice, advises great caution in applying restorative justice in cases of domestic violence. His experience being that "restorative approaches have the greatest impact in more severe cases."[27] Family is the smallest unit but the most essential unit of a healthy society propels us to think of domestic violence as a severe case. Mention may be made of the case of the United States where owing to domestic violence "every year more than million women visit physicians and hospital emergency rooms for treatment after having been beaten by their partner...Over 3 million children per year observe this violence and are subsequently more than six time likely to commit suicide and 50% more likely to abuse drugs and alcohol than children who do not witness such violence."[28]

The story of restoration dates back to God's initiative of justifying sinners out of his infinite reconciling love. Justification as primarily concerned with "being made righteous" before God when applied to DV concerns with making both victim and offender "righteous" before God and each other with the renewal of behavior and outlook This idea of God puts in perspective the rationality of *social constructionism* whereby we acknowledge that there is nothing that is essentially nature or permanent but that much of our perceived human characteristics are created by hosts

26 Zehr, *Restorative Justice*, 28-38.

27 Ibid.

28 Summers and Hoffman, *Domestic Violence*, xiv.

of factors around the person and community and that all things can be changed for the better. Such a standpoint frees both the victims and the offenders from being stereotyped to the extent that they get stuck to the identity of "victim"/ "perpetrator". When God chose to restore the cracks between Him and the world, He does so with a reconciling love in order to accomplish a purpose that changes everyone who is touched by it. Victims and offenders of DV alike can experience changes within themselves and in their relationships so that they are not simply "victim" and "perpetrator" but people in renewed relationship; people who have surmounted devastation of DV; and people who have "protective marks" (Genesis 4:15) of the omnipotent God who lavishes power on all His children to flee from the evil of DV.

Conclusion: The Communal Life of the Church

Faced with complex issues especially linked to domestic violence, the church today finds itself in a challenging and yet privileged position in sense of being able to influence positive changes in family and intimate relationships. We can agree with Beste, who holds that Christians "can be collaborators with God in the affirmation and nurturance of one another's graced freedom. Insofar as this intersubjective nature of freedom characterizes our self-understanding it can sharpen consciences, making it increasingly difficult to deny, minimize, or be apathetic about the prevalence of interpersonal harm among us and its devastating effects."[29] She connects God's grace with human freedom and concludes that God's grace *directly* enables "person's freedom to love God and neighbor."[30] This grace is manifested in His reconciling love and lived by believers in freely yet gratefully being in constant state of relationship with God and with each other.

The essay concludes with the conviction that in order for DV to end, it must first of all become a community concern – church as well as civil societies - and secondly, the restorative process must be both victim-offender centered.

29 Jennifer Erin Beste, *God and the Victim: Traumatic Intrusions on Grace and Freedom* (New York, Oxford University Press, 2007), 111.

30 Ibid., 111-12

11

Integrated Strategies and Interventions to Resist Domestic Violence Against Women

Kaholi Zhimomi[1]

Domestic violence is a global issue that needs global response. It is sustained by the principles of men as superior to women and is culturally institutionalized since history. While examining the gender based violence at homes and intimate relationship, cultural and economic outlook of women cannot be disregarded. Women are forced to accept this reality of violence in their lives because of the stigma and how they are placed in the order of life itself. Domestic violence in intimate relationship may be constructed as any kind of physical, emotional, sexual, psychological and financial abuse of women. This kind of abuse is increasingly coming to the attention of the international forum as a human rights violation, requiring state or government interventions. An integrated strategies and interventions have become necessary to resist domestic violence against women. People, individual groups, governments, national and international bodies working on strategic planning is increasingly faced with several challenges as domestic violence is a complex problem and there is no single strategy that will work in all situations. Domestic violence in one area may differ from another area depending on the societal contexts, and the strategy may vary in measure as to how the

1 Dr. Kaholi Zhimomi was former Assistant Editor of Baptist News, CBCNEI, Guwahati. Presently, she is Assistant Professor at the United Theological College, Bangalore.

particular community sanctions it. Keeping in mind the nature of violence as a weapon against women, a comprehensive and integrated framework of strategies and interventions should be designed.

Strategies and Interventions

There are varied and multi-layered responses to domestic violence which need to be considered in the overall struggle for gender justice. The strategies can be categorized as to those that seek to prevent/ eradicate domestic violence and those that react/respond to such instances which can be further outlined to their target groups and their expected outcomes. Five underlying principles should guide all strategies and interventions attempting to address domestic violence:

(i) Prevention
(ii) Protection
(iii) Early intervention
(iv) Rebuilding the lives of victim-survivors
(v) Accountability[2]

1. Developing Strategies through Research and Documentation

Research and documenting the nature and extent of violence of any kind is the very first step towards countering domestic violence. Analyzing the violence and an understanding of the use and limitations of the legal system will make possible to develop preventive strategies to be used by the field staff and social workers of the organizations.[3] Violence occurs due to several reasons by which both men and women become victims. It comes in the form of religious fundamentalism, lack of openness, lack of secular spirit, eco-injustice, globalization which brings inequality, poverty and militarization. Violence is also manifested in the discrimination of people on the basis of gender,

---

2 "Domestic Violence against Women and Girls," *Innocenti Digest*, No. 6 (June 2000), 15

3 Veena Poonacha, "On the Fringes of Human Rights Discourse: Violence against Women in Intimate Relationships," in *Family Violence in India: Human Rights, Issues, Actions and International Comparisons*, edited by Swati Shirwadkar (New Delhi: Rawat Publications, 2009), 25.

color, creed, caste, race and ethnicity.[4] Women are the worst affected by any kind of violence. This cultural violence is based on patriarchal system of domination and control. Culture has legitimized all kinds of violence against women. Violence therefore destroys the humanhood of a woman. It has affected the lives of millions of women worldwide.[5]

There are different kinds of violence against women such as domestic violence, child marriage and discrimination by employers which occurs in all the countries both developed and developing. Traditional practices of different cultures subjugate women in their own various capacities. This kind of violence differs from culture to culture. Violence against women in family is not only enveloping various cultures, classes and caste but it is deeply embedded and contributes to the low status of women with all the constitutional and human rights guaranteed to women in many countries today.[6] There is also the system of Female Genital Mutilation which hampers women and girl child. According to the World Health Organization, approximately 85 million to 115 million girls and women undergo some form of female genital mutilation and suffer from its adverse health effects. Each year, three million girls are subjected to the practice in Africa. In November 2012, the United Nations (U.N.) passed a resolution condemning female genital mutilation as harmful to women and girls and encouraged member states to take measures to ban the practice. It was the first time the General Assembly's human rights committee addressed the problem.[7]

In the Asian countries there is another kind of violence committed by the parents themselves through the preference of boy child. Many women in these countries choose to abort when

---

4 *Overcoming Violence*, edited by Samsom Prabhakar (Bangalore: SATHRI/BTESSC, 2004), v.

5 Aruna Gnanadason, "Women: Violence and Non-Violence," in *Violence/Non Violence*, edited by Jesudoss (Madras: Gurukul, 1989), 3f.

6 V. S. Elizabeth, "Violence against women in the family: A Human rights violations?" in *Family Violence in India: Human Rights, Issues, Actions and International Comparisons*, edited by Swati Shirwadkar (New Delhi: Rawat Publications, 2009), 144.

7 http://www.stopvaw.org/violence_against_the_girl_child

expecting daughters. Genetic testing for sex selection has become a big business in India. Therefore women groups in India have been protesting against such clinics. There is also dowry related violence based in the traditional set of many societies. Payment of dowry to the groom has been a common practice since generations in some parts of the world. Women are violated because of non-payment of dowry or because of less payment. In India, many women are burnt to death just because of dowry- related issues.[8]

Rape is another violence which has disturbed the lives of many women. It can happen anywhere, whether at home or in public areas at night or during day time leaving women and girl children vulnerable at any time and place. J. L. Gupta quotes June Hopkins, "rape is a sexual expression of power and anger. It is motivated more by retaliatory and compensatory motives than sexual ones and it is a prelude, sexual act is complex and multi-determined." Gupta commented that rape is the most "calculated, cold blooded, deliberate and heinous of crimes."[9] Sexual abuse within marriages and office which are mounting in figures are also violence although sexual abuse at home within marriage is not considered a crime in many countries. A wife is expected to submit to the desires of her husband. Women are also sexually harassed at work place and public transport. But many of these crimes go unnoticed and unreported. Many women are also forced into prostitution by their parents, husbands or boyfriends. Trafficking in women and girl child has also increased in numbers especially in Asian countries. This is a well-organized industry which is victimizing the women.[10]

There is also violence perpetrated by States such as the Custodial violence. Women held in custody are usually raped in police detention centers as reported by Amnesty International. Violence against women in situations of armed conflict is one of the major offences on women. Women and girl children are usually raped by soldiers during conflicts. Rape is used as weapons of war and

8 Jyotsna Mishra, *Women and Human Rights* (Delhi: Kalpaz Publications, 2000), 8ff.

9 J. L Gupta, *Challenge to the Fair Sex: Indian Women, Problems, Plights and Progress* (Delhi: Gyan Publishing House, 1988), 18.

10 Jyotsna Mishra, *Women and Human Rights,* 11f.

as a tool for ethnic cleansing. The Japanese soldiers used "comfort women" another name for sexual slavery. Violence against refugees and displaced women is also rampant in conflict or war torn areas. Women and children form the majority of the refugee populations all over the world. They become victims of rape, abuse by military, bandit groups, male refuges and rival ethnic groups.[11]

2. Strategic Planning through Social Action

2.1. *Empowering of Women: Education and Economic Stability*

In order to prevent violence a social action on neighborhood vigilance and the creation of new socio-economic options by employment opportunities and skill training for women likely to be targets of domestic violence in a necessity. Empowering of women in the knowledge of their rights and enabling them to access information about various government welfare and schemes is essential.[12] Women need to be empowered through education, employment opportunities, legal literacy, and right to inheritance. Education will enhance a woman's knowledge of her basic rights and a skill based training where she can generate income to sustain herself. Education will inform women of the agencies which are emerging to support their rights (legal, para-legal, constitutional and informal community structures) and also enlighten them of the various schemes and programmes established by the government and non-governmental organizations to help equip women to lead a monetarily secured lives.[13] Human rights education and information regarding domestic violence should be provided to them because this is a matter of their absolute rights. Integrated supportive services, legal intervention and redress should be made available in situations of domestic violence. Assistance to help women rebuild and recover their lives after violence

---

11 Jyotsna Mishra, *Women and Human Rights*, 14f.

12 Veena Poonacha, "On the Fringes of Human Rights Discourse: Violence Against Women in Intimate Relationships," 26.

13 Medha Bisht, "Women as Victims of Violence: Emerging Nuances and Interventions," *Women's Link*, 10/4 (October- December 2004), 18.

should be part of the intervention strategy, including counseling, relocation, credit support, and employment.[14]

2.2. *Victim-survivors Action Plan*

Shelter homes, short stay homes, free legal aid, counseling and child care facilities need to be made available in different areas to help facilitate effected women. Residential centers should be opened to provide psychological and financial support for victims. There is also a need for training of professional workers on issues relating to the victims health, identity rebuilding and medical care.[15] India still lacks facilities for women but efforts though the state-sponsored Mahila Samakhya Programme has made attempts to prevent violence through the empowerment of women. It has established self-help groups at village levels to help the poor-rural women to acquire necessary knowledge and self-confidence. The National Commission for Women in order to help women raise their family cases has established *Parivarik Mahila Lok Adalat* (family courts for Women) in collaboration with the Non Governmental Organizations (NGOs) even in remote areas with the help of the state legal aid and advisory bodies. In 1984 with the rise of violence against women the Central Social Welfare Board (CSWB), a semi-autonomous body, through the State Social Welfare Advisory Boards (SSWABs) established the Family Counselling Cells (FCCs) attached to selected police stations to provide preventive, referral and rehabilitative services to women and children survivors of violence.[16]

The Protection of Women from Domestic Violence Act, 2005, Domestic Violence Bill (Bill No. 116 of 2005) which came into force on October 26, 2006 has been enacted to provide more effective protection to the rights of the women guaranteed under article 14, 15, 16 and 21 of the Constitution to prevent unbearable acts against women. This legal law enforced protection of Indian women

---

14 "Domestic Violence against Women and Girls," 15.

15 Anoop Kumari Bhartiya, "Domestic Violence Against Women: An Overview, " in *Domestic Violence against Women in India,* edited by A. K. Singh; S. P. Singh and S. P. Pandey (Gurgaon: Madhav Books, 2009), 180.

16 Veena Poonacha, "On the Fringes of Human Rights Discourse: Violence against Women in Intimate Relationships," p. 26ff.

in many ways have boosted up the confidence of many women in India leading them to voice out their exploitation under domestic and intimate relationships and checked themselves from further evils upon them though great lacunae still exist in fulfilling many of the basic features of the act.[17]

Self Help Groups have emerged as the best and the most efficient means of organizing women for their empowerment. These SHGs are helping women across the country in skill formulation. It was primarily for credits and savings activities but their broader scope and goal is social and economic independence of women. With the social and economic empowerment women would begin to be aware of their rights and make equal partners in the family decision making. According to the study undertaken by the Programme Support and Research Unit at the Development Support Team (DST) on cases like, "Women's Empowerment through SHGs: A Case Study of DST (1999)," it has indicated that these groups could become an important and essential medium to address the issue of domestic violence.[18]

3. Awareness Generation: An Integrated Intervention

3.1. *The Local Community*

The awareness generation program requires efforts to raise community opinion against domestic violence and the mobilization of the entire community to oppose violence and support the woman.[19] A systematic effort has to be made to listen to the voices of grassroot women and survivors of domestic violence, and to incorporate solutions they have to offer. Their perspectives will provide valuable lessons in making programmes and services effective and targeted to their needs. There is a need for community-based support mechanisms

---

17 Rattan Singh & Mehak Ahuja, "Domestic Violence in India: A Milestone in Protection of Women," in *Family Violence in India* edited by Subhash Chandra Singh (New Delhi: Serials Pub, 2010), 93f.

18 Milind Bokil, "Ending Domestic Violence," in *Family Violence in India: Human Rights, Issues, Actions and International Comparisons*, edited by Swati Shirwadkar (New Delhi: Rawat Publications, 2009), 240f.

19 Veena Poonacha, "On the Fringes of Human Rights Discourse: Violence against Women in Intimate Relationships," 26.

to resolve issues of conflict. The local community needs to be mobilized to oppose domestic violence and take actions on any kind of gender based violence in the community. The society should not lay in contentment but be active group in intervening and building up education system to prepare the local community. Community information and education programmes regarding the nature and unacceptability of domestic violence should be developed. Many traditional cultural practices, such as the Female Genital Mutilation, dowry system, which impede the integrity of women should be re-examined and challenged.[20]

A special community project by the Domestic Abuse Intervention Project (DAIP) is a well-known Community Intervention Projects (CIP) that has been a model for communities in Minnesota, Colorado, California, Wisconsin, and Washington. DAIP has been successful in negotiating key agreements with intervening agencies by meeting with representatives from each agency separately and holding inter-agency meetings to discuss policy and programmatic issues after initial agreements have been reached. CIP is an advocacy to focus on reforming, improving, and coordinating institutional responses to domestic violence within a community. They are distinguished from coordinating councils and criminal justice-based reform projects in that they are non-profit agencies that are external to the criminal justice system and rooted in the battered women's movement. There are eight key components of community intervention projects that has been identified: (1) creating a philosophical approach that centralizes victim safety; (2) developing polices and protocols that enhance victim safety; (3) enhancing networking among service providers; (4) building monitoring and tracking systems that strengthen system accountability; (5) advocating for battered women within the criminal justice system and the broader community to insure a supportive infrastructure; (6) providing sanctions and rehabilitation opportunities for abusers; (7) undoing the harm violence to women does to children; and (8) evaluating the coordinated community

20 "Domestic Violence against Women and Girls," 15.

response for victim safety and offender accountability.[21] This model of CIP can be used as a base work to different community projects in different areas according to the special needs of the particular regions.

3.2. *Role of Women's Organization*

Over the years women's organizations have been voicing out against the injustice against women within their own family circles. They have played significant role in liberating women who suffer within the bondage of marriage. These women organizations have empowered women with confidence to voice out against family violence and seek interventions for combating abuse. They have been instrumental in pushing forward effective implementations of the existing policies and sensitizing the law enforcing machinery to be proactive. Women organizations have been effective in giving victim-survivors a voice during various hearings and private witnesses. They sought to empower women through human rights, education, credit programmes and linking women to larger networks. [22]

Women's advocacy has pressed the formal sectors (legal and judicial system, criminal justice system, and the health sector) to initiate counter-response to the needs of women who suffer violence. They have been demanding for policy change and institutional mechanisms to be set up in all the system whether in the form of legal reform, training of police, or providing shelter to women and their children. The most important role they play is monitoring and accountability role, in partnerships with governments sectors.[23]

---

21 Duraipandi Mavoothu, "Domestic Violence: An Assessment of Global Scenario," in *Family Violence in India* edited by Subhash Chandra Singh (New Delhi: Serials Pub, 2010), 41.

22 R. Indira, "Battered and Bound in Their Own Homes: Does Family Violence Have an Answer?" in *Family Violence in India: Human Rights, Issues, Actions and International Comparisons*, edited by Swati Shirwadkar, (New Delhi: Rawat Publications, 2009), 280.

23 "Domestic Violence against Women and Girls," 16.

3.3. *International Organizations*

International organizations such as the United Nations, its bodies and specialized agencies, the World Bank, and the Inter-American Development Bank have placed the issue of violence against women in their agendas. The United Nations in its final declaration of the World Conference of Human Rights recognized the issues of female infanticide, mass rape in armed conflict, sex tourism, circumcision practices, and domestic violence as universal and fundamental human rights at the international level. Gender violence was also recognized as a fundamental violation of human rights. In line with this development, the International Convention on Population and Development at Cairo in 1994, the Fourth World Conference on Women in Beijing, 1995 also accepted the principle of women's rights as human rights and created the alternative framework through which violence against women in private and public realms could be understood as an extension of human rights violations. Another conference which focused on gender violence was the Rome Statute of the International Criminal Court (ICC) adopted in July 17, 1998 which took into court's jurisdiction any kind of violence against women both in the private and public domain. One of the notable changes in ICC was also the fair representation of male and female judges during selection process.[24]

United Nations Children's Fund (UNICEF) works with different partners to address domestic violence in many countries. Examples include: facilitating creation of Bolivia's National Plan for the Prevention of and Eradication of Violence Against Women (1994) and the adoption of Law 1674 against Family or Domestic Violence (1995); work with the National Jordanian Television to develop TV spots on violence against women; and support for the development of an active movement against gender based violence in Afghanistan and other countries in South Asia. The Trust Fund in Support of Actions to Eliminate Violence against Women, established at UNIFEM in 1996 by a UN General Assembly resolution, has

24 Medha Bisht, "Women as Victims of Violence: Emerging Nuances and Interventions," *Women's Link*, 10/4 (October- December 2004), 16.

supported innovative projects around the world that address all forms of gender-based violence.[25]

The UN Development Fund for Women (UNIFEM) has launched a campaign in the Kenyan capital Naiborbi to organize people around the world to take part in a drive to stop the pandemic of violence against women. The UN Secretary-General-led campaign UNITE to End Violence against has been advocated to reach out to 1 million a year. This is a high profile global effort and action reaching out to students at schools, volunteering at local shelters, advocating for legislation or donating funds towards programmes that protect women and girls from violence. With the augmentation of violence against women and girls commercial companies are also getting themselves involved for this cause. The luxury watch manufacturer OMEGA, with the collaboration of the UNIFEM Goodwill Ambassador, Nicole Kidman, has announced a grant of $50,000 for the first 50,000 proceedings to be donated to the organizations working for women.[26]

World Health Organization (WHO) has recognized violence against women as a public health and human rights concern which ignored slows down the growth of development itself. It has coordinated a multi-country study on women's health and domestic violence, which aims to develop methodologies to measure violence against women and its health consequences cross-culturally in different countries. WHO has been the major forerunner in this issue in conducting research and outreach in various countries. The WHO Multi-country Study on Women's Health and Domestic Violence against Women has contributed to thwart violence against women by raising public awareness and working toward prevention in many countries. Multi-country Study is a model for conducting statistical research in the area of violence and its effects on the health on women. WHO Multi-country Study in collaboration with the International Violence Against Women Survey (IVAWS) has made an important scientific and methodology of interviewing women about violence in cross- cultural settings. They have made highly

25 "Domestic Violence against Women and Girls," 19.

26 Duraipandi Mavoothu, "Domestic Violence: An Assessment of Global Scenario," 36.

developed and well-tested tools for researchers and community activists seeking for conducting quantitative surveys in local settings. Various WHO study were significant as they were able to provide estimates of the magnitudes and nature of violence against women in ten countries. The WHO has also launched a Global Campaign for Violence Prevention to advocate public health approach to targeting violence at the national level. In the 2002 publication of the *World Report on Violence and Health*, WHO makes nine recommendations for action to reduce violence:

1. Create, implement and monitor a national action plan for violence prevention
2. Enhance capacity for collecting data on violence
3. Define priorities for, and support research on, the causes, consequences, costs and prevention of violence
4. Promote primary prevention responses
5. Strengthen responses for victims of violence
6. Integrate violence prevention into social and educational policies, and thereby promote gender and social equality
7. Increase collaboration and exchange of information on violence prevention
8. Promote and monitor adherence to international treaties, laws and other mechanisms to protect human rights
9. Seek practical, internationally agreed responses to the global drugs trade and the global arms trade[27]

3.4. *Religious Leaders: Involvement of the Church*

The church must re-examine the theological messages it communicates in light of the experiences of victims of domestic violence and sexual abuse. They must treat with extreme care the important, but often-misused, concepts of suffering, and forgiveness. Situations of violence and abuse exist in families in virtually every congregation; tragically, no church or community is exempt. Christian families and communities are not immune to any kind of violence. The church

27 Holly Johnson, Natalia Ollus & Sami Nevala, *Violence against Women: An International Perspective* (New York: Springer Science+Business Media, LLC, 2008), 176f.

is therefore challenged to listen to the stories of victims and survivors and assist in giving guidance to those church members experiencing domestic violence and sexual abuse especially children. The church should not only be a sanctuary for spiritual retreat but a refuge for people who are hurting and a place of healing and comfort. It should provide a platform for addressing these issues. Christians should be in forefront voicing out against these issues like domestic violence and sexual abuse. The church should create a climate of openness, acceptance, and safety that encourages victims to speak of their pain and seek relief and healing. The clergy and lay church leaders need to work along with the community agencies or Non Governmental Organizations (NGO) on prevention strategies and to provide for the physical, emotional, and spiritual needs of children, victims, offenders, and other family members. There should also be policies and procedures for keeping children and vulnerable adults safe from abuse in church facilities and programs. The church from time to time should undertake new programs ecumenically or as part of a community association. There is also a need for peer support groups for spouses, adults who were sexually abused as children, and for rape victims. A trained resource person or professional counselor should be appointed for essential counseling and assistances for any children or church members needing assistance. The church as whole should re-examine, and change if necessary, scriptural and theological messages, cultures, and traditions that legalize violence or abuse.

Violence of any form is always spiritually destructive. It threatens self-respect and mutual trust, giving rise to feelings of personal and social powerlessness. Violence destroys our human capacity to create and transform community, both interpersonal and political. Our call, therefore, as a church should be to end violence of any kind whether in public or private domain. The church must be the centre of breaking the silence against any kind of injustice or violence existing in the church or the society. No violence against children or be it anybody women or adult is justifiable. Violence against weaker group of people is preventable but it all need to start by addressing factors that give rise to violence and taking measures to ensure the safety of the victims. The churches in Northeast India should be a platform for creating awareness of violence and abuse in any form. The churches need to take measures in their respective parish for women and children development and protection for in doing so we are in the process of building tomorrow's church, society and nation.

Conclusion

Violence against women is a major issue of concern for every country both developed and underdeveloped although it may vary in dynamics depending on the areas and context. Whether it is human trafficking, female infanticides, dowry, rapes, abuses, family violence, domestic violence, or any type of gendered based violence, it is a disturbing truth that women all over the world exist in this reality. Efforts are being made at various levels to eradicate this cruel human rights violations but despite of all the attempts made by at the local and national levels violence of women continue to increase. Therefore it has become necessary to research into the structure that exists. Violence will continue as long as the power relations between a man and woman are unequal in terms of decision-making, both in private and public sphere. There is also the social stigma of caste and tribes which elevates the cases of violence against women. Until and unless the power struggle/relation at any level which begins to deprive and discriminate be re-examined violence cannot be controlled. There is also an urgent need for sensitizing and involving the community through various programs against social evils of domestic violence. Quality and higher education need to be made available to all both boy child and girl child. Women's economic empowerment, legal status of women requires to be improved. Mass awareness and monitoring by various groups both government and non-governmental organizations like the social workers, health care units, educational institutions, legal fraternity and police is an imperative need to crab violence against women.

Violence against women is not foreseeable but can be shunned if dealt with correctly. Women's lives in the families, societies and communities traumatized by violence can be defended. There still is a great scope to enlarge strategies and interventions to tackle these social evils as the present tactics presented is exhaustible in itself. The worldwide understanding support system is emergent and to a great extent constructive experience has already been gained. If each individual, family, society, community, group, organization government and private continues to build upon these strategies and interventions and use it as practical tools, violence against women particularly domestic violence could be eradicated at certain point. To absolutely eliminate domestic violence people should be willing to instigate, support, cooperate, innovate and dedicate to the one sole cause of preventing violence.

Bibliography

Books, Articles, Websites and Works Cited Frequently in Alphabetical Order

Adams, Carol J. & Mary M. Fortune. *Violence against Women and Children: A Christian Theological Sourcebook.* New York: The Continuum Publishing Company, 1998.

Anderson, Hubert; D. S. Browning, I. S. Evison, M. S. V. Leeuwen. Eds. *The Family Handbook.* Louisville, KY: Westminster John Knox Press, 1998.

Aulen, Gustav. *Christus Victor: An Historical Study of the Three Main Types of the Idea of the Atonement.* London: SPCK, 2010 [1931].

Baker, David L. "The Humanisation of Slavery in Old Testament Law." In *Ethics in Brief* 12/4(2007).

Baltazar, Stella. "Domestic Violence in Indian Perspective." In *Women Resisting Violence.* Eds. Mary John Mananzan, et al. Eugene, Oregon: Wipf and Stock Publishers, 2004.

Bart, Pauline B. & Eileen Geil Moran. Eds. *Violence against Women: The Bloody Footprints.* California: Sage, 1993.

Bechtel, Lyn M. "What if Dinah is not Raped? (Genesis 34)." In *JSOT* 62 (1994).

Beste, Jennifer Erin. *God and the Victim: Traumatic Intrusions on Grace and Freedom.* New York: Oxford University Press, 2007.

Bhartiya, Anoop Kumari. "Domestic Violence against Women: An Overview." In *Domestic Violence against Women in India.* Edited by A. K. Singh; S. P. Singh and S. P. Pandey. Gurgaon: Madhav Books, 2009.

Bisht, Medha. "Women as Victims of Violence: Emerging Nuances and Interventions." In *Women's Link* 10/4 (October-December 2004).

Bokil, Milind. "Ending Domestic Violence." In *Family Violence in India: Human Rights, Issues, Actions and International Comparisons*. Edited by Swati Shirwadkar. New Delhi: Rawat Publications, 2009.

Brown, R. E. *The Epistles of John: Translation with Introduction, Notes and Commentary*, ABC, Vol. 30. New York: Doubleday, 1982.

Bultmann, R. *The Johannine Epistles*. Trans. R. Philip O'Hara, Lane C. McGaughy and Robert W. Funk, Hermeneia. Philadelphia: Fortress, 1973, German 1967.

Cardoza, Freddy. "Crisis on the Doorstep." *A Theology for Family Ministries*. Edited by Michael & Michelle Anthony. Nashville, TN: B. & H. Academic, 2011.

Chima, Harneet. "The Efficacy of Laws in Preventing Domestic Violence." In *Crime and Women*. Ed. Ruchi Ghosh Dastidar.

Conway, Helen L. *Domestic Violence and the Church*. Secunderabad: OM Books, 2003.

Cooper-White, Pamela. *The Cry of Tamar: Violence against Women and the Church's Response*. Philadelphia: Fortress Press, 1995.

Deb, Sibnath. *Children in Agony: A Source Book*. New Delhi: Concept Publishing Company, 2006.

Dobash, R. E. and R. P. Dobash. "Wives: The Appropriate Victims of Domestic Violence." In *Victimology: An International Journal* 2 (1978).

"Domestic Violence against Women and Girls." *Innocenti Digest*, No. 6 (June 2000).

Domestic Violence in India: A Summary Report of a Multi-Site Household Survey, 2003, International Centre for Research on Women, Washington D.C.

Driver, Samuel R. *A Critical and Exegetical Commentary: Deuteronomy*. 3rd Edition. Edinburgh: T & T Clark, 1965.

Elizabeth, V. S. "Violence against Women in the Family: A Human Rights Violations?" In *Family Violence in India: Human Rights, Issues, Actions and International Comparisons*. Edited by Swati Shirwadkar. New Delhi: Rawat Publications, 2009.

Evans, Mary J. "Women." In *Dictionary of the Old Testament Historical Books.* Edited by Bill T. Arnold & H. G. M. Williamson. Downers Grove: IVP, 2009.

Ferguson, Sinclair B. "Preaching the Atonement." In *The Glory of the Atonement: Biblical, Historical and Practical Perspectives.* Edited by Charles E. Hill and Frank A. James III. Downers Grove, IL: InterVarsity Press, 2004.

Figes, Eva. *Patriarchal Attitudes: Women in Society*. London: Virago, 1978.

Fiorenza, Elizabeth Schüssler. *Bread Not Stone: The Challenge of Feminist Biblical Interpretation.* Boston: Beacon Press, 1985.

Foucault, Michel. *Power/Knowledge: Selected Interviews and Other Writings.* Edited by Colin Gardon. New York: Pantheon, 1980.

Friesen, Delores and Mary Shamshoian, "Peacemaking in the Family: A Systematic View of Domestic Violence." In Frampton F. Fox, ed. *Violence and Peace: Creating a Culture of Peace in the Contemporary Context of Violence.* Papers from the 15th Annual Centre for Mission Studies Consultation, UBS, Pune. Pune: CMS & Bangalore: ATC, 2010.

Gill, D. W. "Violence." In D. J. Atkinson, et al., eds. *New Dictionary of Christian Ethics and Pastoral Theology.* Downers Grove, Illinois: InterVarsity Press, 1995.

Gnanadason, Aruna. "Women: Violence and Non-Violence." In *Violence/Non Violence.* Edited by Jesudoss. Madras: Gurukul, 1989.

Gravett, Sandie. "Reading 'Rape.' In the Hebrew Bible: A Consideration of Language." In *JSOT* 28/3 (2004).

Gupta, J. L. *Challenge to the Fair Sex: Indian Women, Problems, Plights and Progress.* Delhi: Gian Publishing House, 1988.

Hayward, Finney Ruth. *Breaking the Earthenware Jar: Lessons from South-Asia to End Violence against Women and Girls.* Kathmandu, Nepal: UNICEF, 2000.

Hearn, Jeff. *The Violence's of Men.* Sage: London, 1998.

Heise, Lori; Mary Ellsberg, Megan Gottemoeller. *Ending Violence against Women: Population Reports,* Series L No.11. Baltimore,

Maryland: John Hopkins University School of Public Health, Population Information Program, 1999.

Hirsch, Mariam F. *Women and Violence.* New York: Van Nostrand Reinhold, 1981.

Hnuni, R. L. "Vision for Women in North East India." In *Transforming Theology for Empowering Women: A Theological and Hermeneutical Reflection in the context of North East India.* Edited by R. L. Hnuni. Jorhat: Women Study Centre, Eastern Theological College, 1999.

Horam, M. *Naga Polity*. Delhi: B.R., 1975.

Hunter, Rosemary. "Having Her Day in Court? Violence, Legal Remedies and Consent." In *Innovative Responses to Sexual and Domestic Violence.* Edited by Jan Breckenridge and Lesley Laing. St Leonards NSW, Australia: Allen & Unwin, 1999.

Imchen, Narola. *Women in Church and Society: The Story of Ao Naga Women.* Jorhat: Eastern Theological College, 2001.

Indira, R. "Battered and Bound in Their Own Homes: Does Family Violence Have an Answer?" In *Family Violence in India: Human Rights, Issues, Actions and International Comparisons.* Edited by Swati Shirwadkar. New Delhi: Rawat Publications, 2009.

Jacobs, Mignon R. "Toward an Old Testament Theology of Concern for the Underprivileged." In *Reading the Hebrew Bible for a New Millennium: Form, Concept and Theological Perspective.* Edited by Wonil Kim et al. Harrisburg, PA: Trinity Press International, 2000.

Jager, Uli, et al. *Fostering Civic and Nonviolent Education in Jordan.* Berlin: Bergh of Foundation, 2014.

Jamir, L. Imsutoshi. "Globalization of Culture: Challenges for Doing Theology in Asia." In *The Journal of Theologies and Cultures in Asia* 2 (2003): 167-182.

Jamir, L. Imsutoshi. "Morality of Inter-subjectivity: Toward Inclusive Tribal Community," *Journal of Tribal Studies,* 16/2, (2011):16-31.

Jamir, Talitemjen and A. Lanunungsang. *Naga Society and Culture: A Case Study of the Ao Naga Society and Culture.* Lumami: Nagaland University, Tribal Research Centre, 2005.

Johann, S. L. and F. Osanka, eds. *Representing Battered Women Who Kill.* Springfield, Ill.: Thomas, 1989.

Johnson, Holly; Natalia Ollus & Sami Nevala. *Violence against Women: An International Perspective.* New York: Springer Science+Business Media, LLC, 2008.

Johnson, Janet Elise. *Gender Violence in Russia.* Bloomington, Indiana: Indiana University Press, 2009.

Just Die Quietly: Domestic Violence and Women's Vulnerability to HIV in Uganda, Human Rights. New York: Watch, Ny, 2003.

Koala Jones-Warsaw. "Toward a Womanist Hermeneutic: A Reading of Judges 19-21." In *Feminist Companion to Judges.* Edited by Athalya Brenner. Sheffield: Sheffield Academic Press, 1993.

Krug, Etienne, Linda Dalhberg; James Mercy, et al. eds. *World Report on Violence and Health.* Switzerland, Geneva: WHO, 2002.

Levy, Barrie. *Women and Violence.* Berkeley, CA: Seal Press, 2008.

Luck, William F. *Divorce and Remarriage: Recovering the Biblical View.* San Francisco: Harper & Row, 1987.

Luithni, Shimreichon. "Naga Women: A Struggle for Human Rights." In Diana Vinding. Ed. *Indigenous Women: The Right to a Voice: International Work Group for Indigenous Affairs.* Copenhagen: n.p. 1998.

Mathew, Suseela. *Breaking the Barriers.* Bangalore: Christian Institute for the Study of Religion and Society, n. d.

Mavoothu, Duraipandi. "Domestic Violence: An Assessment of Global Scenario." In *Family Violence in India.* Edited by Subhash Chandra Singh. New Delhi: Serials Pub, 2010.

May, Scottie; Beth Posterski, Catherine Stonehouse, and Linda Cannell. *Children Matter: Celebrating Their Place in the Church, Family and Community* (Grand Rapids, MI: Wm. B. Eerdmans Publishing Company, 2005), 152-153.

Mayes, A. D. H. *Deuteronomy.* Grand Rapids: Eerdmans, 1981.

McGoldrick, Monica, Mary Anne Broken Nose, Mildred Potenza. "Violence and the Family Life Cycle." In *The Expanded Family Life Cycle: Individual, Family, and Social Perspectives.* Third Edition. Edited by Betty Carter and Monica McGoldrick. Boston: Allyn and Bacon, 1999.

Merrill, Eugene H. *Deuteronomy.* Nashville: Broadman & Holman, 1994.

Merton, Thomas. *Faith and Violence: Christian Teaching and Christian Practice.* Notre Dame, Indiana: University of Notre Dame, 1976, 1968.

Mishra, Jyotsna. *Women and Human Rights.* Delhi: Kalpaz Publications, 2000.

Mitchell, Hinckley G., John Merlin Powis Smith & Julius A. Bewer. *A Critical and Exegetical Commentary on Haggai, Zechariah, Malachi and Jonah.* Edinburgh: T&T Clark, 1912.

Nasrin, Taslima. "At the Back of Progress." In *Musings on Vital Issues.* Ed. P. J. George. Chennai: Orient Blackswan Private Limited, 2010.

Phillips, Anthony. "Another Look at Adultery." In *SOT* 20(1981), 9.

Phillips, Anthony. *Ancient Israel's Criminal Law: A New Approach to the Decalogue.* New York: Schocken, 1970.

Poonacha, Veena. "On the Fringes of Human Rights Discourse: Violence against Women in Intimate Relationships." In *Family Violence in India: Human Rights, Issues, Actions and International Comparisons.* Edited by Swati Shirwadkar. New Delhi: Rawat Publications, 2009.

Prabhakar, Samsom. Ed. *Overcoming Violence.* Bangalore: SATHRI/ BTESSC, 2004.

Pressler, Carolyn. "Sexual Violence and Deuteronomic Law." *A Feminist Companion to Exodus and Deuteronomy.* Edited by Athalya Brenner. Sheffield: Sheffield Academic Press, 1994.

Roy, Maria. Ed. *Battered Women: A Psychological Study of Domestic Violence.* New York: Van Nostrand Reinhold, 1977.

Sarkar, Ratna. "Gender Inequality in India: An Overview." In *Social Defence* 53/152 (April 2002).

Schnackenburg, R. *The Johannine Epistles: A Commentary.* Trans. T. Reginald and I. Fuller. Kent: Burns and Oates, 1992, German 1984.

Schnelle, U. *Theology of the New Testament.* Trans. M. E. Boring. Michigan: Baker Academic, 2007.

Schroer, Silvia. "We Will Know Each Other by Our Fruits: Feminist Exegesis and the Hermeneutics of Liberation." In *Feminist Interpretation of the Bible and the Hermeneutics of Liberation.* Edited by Silvia Schroer & Sophia Bietenhard. London: Sheffield Academic Press, 2003.

Sen, A. *Resources, Values and Development.* Cambridge: Mass, 1984.

Sharma, Bela Rani. *Women-Marriage, Family, Violence and Divorce.* Jaipur: Mangal Deep, 1997.

Singh, Rattan & Mehak Ahuja. "Domestic Violence in India: A Milestone in Protection of Women." In *Family Violence in India.* Edited by Subhash Chandra Singh. New Delhi: Serials Pub, 2010.

Skjelsbæk, Inger. "Is Femininity Inherently Peaceful? The Construction of Femininity in War." *Gender, Peace and Conflict.* Ed. Inger Skjelbæk and Dan Smith. London/California/New Delhi: SAGE Publications, 2001.

Smalley, S. S. *1, 2, 3 John*, WBC, Vol. 51. Waco, Texas: Word Books, Publisher, 1984.

Strecker, G. *The Letters of John, A Commentary on 1, 2, and 3 John.* Trans. L.M. Maloney, ed. H. Attridge. Minneapolis: Fortress, 1996, German 1989.

Styler, Rebecca. "A Scripture of Their Own: Nineteenth-Century Bible Biography and Feminist Bible Criticism," *Christianity and Literature* 57/1 (Autumn 2007), 65.

Summers, Randal W. and Allan M. Hoffman. Eds. *Domestic Violence: A Global View.* Westport, CT: Greenwood Press, 2002.

Tamez, Elsa. "Women's Rereading of the Bible." In *Feminist Theology from the Third World.* Edited by Ursula King. London: Orbis Book, 1994.

Tifft, Larry L. *Battering Of Women: The Failure of Intervention and the Case for Prevention*. Westview: Boulder, 1993.

Tracy, Steven. "Patriarchy and Domestic Violence: Challenging Common Misconceptions." In *Journal of the Evangelical Theological Society* (2007), 580-583.

Trible, Phyllis. *Texts of Terror.* Philadelphia: Fortress Press, 1984.

Upton, Bridget Gilfillan. "Feminist Theology as Biblical Hermeneutics." *The Cambridge Companion to Feminist Theology.* Edited by Susan Frank Parsons. Cambridge: Cambridge University Press, 2002.

Volf, Miroslav. "Original Crime, Primal Care." In *God and the Victim: Theological Reflections on Evil, Victimization, Justice and Forgiveness.* Edited by Lisa Barnes Lampman. Grand Rapids, MI/ Cambridge, UK: Wm. B. Eerdmans/Neighbors Who Care, 1999.

Wells, Bruce. "Sex, Lies, and Virginal Rape: The Slandered Bride and False Accusation in Deuteronomy." In *JBL 124/1* (2005), 42.

World Development Report: Investing in Health. Oxford/New York: World Bank, 1993.

Zehol, Lucy, ed., *Women in Naga Society.* New Delhi: Regency, 1988.

Webliography

Ankur Kumar, "Domestic Violence in India: Causes, Consequences, and Remedies" http://www.youthkiawaaz.com (accessed on 1/11/2014).

Domestic violence. http:// w3.whosea.org/ Linkfiles/ Reproductive Health Profile domestic.pdf#search=%22NFHS%202% Domestic%20 violence%22.

"Child Maltreatment" http://www.who.int/topics/child_abuse/en/ (accessed on 4/11/2014).

"Domestic Violence and the Child Welfare System." *Bulletin for Professionals*, Oct. 2009, www.childwelfare.gov.

"Domestic Violence in India: The Protection of Women from Domestic Violence Act 2005," http://www.helplinelaw.com/family-law/DVLI/domestic-violence-in-india.html (accessed on 3/11/2014).

http://www.stopvaw.org/violence_against_the_girl_child.

http://www.unhchr.ch/huridocda/huridoca.nsf/(Symbol)/A.RES.48.104.En?Opendocument).

"India tackles domestic violence," BBC News. 27/10/206. Retrieved 25 April 2012.

"Let's Talk Facts About Domestic Violence." American Psychiatric Association. www.soc.iastate. edu/sapp/DomesticViolence.pdf (29/10/2014).

"Protect Domestic Workers from Violence," http://www.hrw.org/news/2008/11/24/ (accessed on 31/10/2014).

Reed, Lorrie C. "Theological Reflection on Domestic Violence," http://reflectiverenewal.blogspot.in/2013/10/theological-reflection-on-domestic.html (accessed on 7/11/2014).

Through Their Eyes: Domestic Violence and Its Impact on Children. Moving Women and Families Forward. www.ywcaworks.org (accessed on 28/10/2014).

"Violence against children, within the family and in schools," www.ohcr.org/EN/HRBodies/CRC/Documents/.../school.pdf (accessed on 3/11/2014).

"What is Domestic Violence? Who is Affected by Domestic . . ." www.domesticviolence.com.au/files/pdf/Info-Book-Final.pdf (accessed on 27/10/2014).

Contributors

A. Tali Ao is Senior Lecturer and HoD of the Department of the New Testament, Clark Theological College, Aolijen.

Atungo Shitri is currently the Secretary, Peace & Justice Ministries, CBCNEI, Guwahati.

Elizabeth Imti is Assistant Professor in the Department of Sociology, Fazl Ali College, Mokokchung.

Eyingbeni Hümtsoe-Nienu is Senior Lecturer in Department of Christian Theology, Clark Theological College, Aolijen.

K. Lallawmzuala is Associate Professor, Department of the Old Testament, Aizawl Theological College, Aizawl.

Kaholi Zhimomi was former Assistant Editor of Baptist News, CBCNEI, Guwahati. Presently, she is Assistant Professor at the United Theological College, Bangalore.

L. Imsutoshi Jamir is Associate Professor, Department of Communication and Director of CCCRC the Clark Theological College, Aolijen.

Meyijungla, a former faculty member of the Witter Theological College, Wokha, presently she is on the staff of Bible Society of India, Shillong.

Mhonyamo Lotha, a former Lecturer at the Clark Theological College, Aolijen, in the Department of History of Christianity, presently he is pursuing his Ph.D. at the Martin Luther Christian University, Shillong.

Razouselie Lasetso is Associate Professor, Department of New Testament, Eastern Theological College, Jorhat.

Toshimenla Jamir is Associate Professor, Department of Sociology, Nagaland University, Lumami.